Table of Contents

Exam Review

The Association of Social Work Boards (ASWB) examination has five tiers of competency—Associates, Bachelors, Master, Advanced Generalist, and Clinical. This exam review covers the areas of the Bachelors level of competency. Please refer to the ASWB Social Work Candidate Licensing Examination Candidate Handbook for information about scheduling the exam. The specific areas and their percentages of use on the actual exam are listed on the chart below.

Bachelors Examination Content Outline
Percent of content

I. Human Development, Diversity, and Behavior in the Environment 27%
Models of human growth and development
Models of human behavior in the social environment
Diversity
Effects of the environment on client system behavior

II. Assessment   28%
Social history and collateral data
Problem identification
Assessment of client system's strengths and challenges
Assessment of addictive behaviors
Assessment of mental and behavioral disorders
Dynamics and indicators of abuse and neglect

III. Direct and Indirect Practice   26%
Indicators and effects of crisis and change
Intervention processes and techniques
Matching intervention with client system needs
Use of collaborative relationships
Documentation
Interviewing
Evidence-based practice

IV. Professional Relationships, Values and Ethics   19%

Ethical responsibility to the client system and profession
Confidentiality
Client's right to self-determination
Professional use of self
Methods of professional development

Review

Review information is meant to be selective rather than comprehensive. Under each heading, you will find specific information that is key to the practice and actual test. Reviewing this snapshot information will aid in memorizing key terms and ideas for the test.

Human Development, Diversity, and Behavior in the Environment

Modern human rights laws are inclined toward cultural diversity. Under the umbrella of cultural diversity are related rights, such as ethnic minority equality, cultural heritage regulations, and non-discrimination. The term for Awareness of cultural diversity within the social work industry is cultural competence.

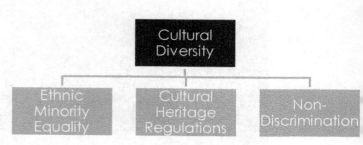

There are nine dimensions of environment related to social work. They are the communities, culture, dyads, families, formal organizations, physical environment, small groups, social institutions and social structure, and social movements. Although this book covers each dimension separately, they are neither independent nor hierarchically ordered.

A social worker's responsibility is to think about and attempt to understand the nature and complexities of the people and situations that are at the center of their practice. Three major aspects of this approach to human behavior are people, environment, and time. It goes without question that each of these aspects cannot be fully understood without grasping how they related to one another. On the next page, you will find a chart labeled figure 1 that illustrates how these separate systems are intertwined.

FIGURE 1

The Individual	Immediate Household	Extended Family	Communal Connections	Larger Society
Age	Family structure	Relationship patterns	Face-to-face links between individual, family, and society	Social, political, economic issues
Gender roles & sexual orientation	Stage of family life cycle	Emotional legacies, themes, secrets, family myths, taboos	Friends and neighbors	Bias based on race or ethinicity
Temperament	Emotional climate			Bias based on class
Developmental or physical disabilities	Boundaries, patterns, and triangles	Loss	Involvement with gov. institutions	Bias based on sexual orientation
Culture, race, ethnicity	Communication patterns	Socioeconomic level & issues	Self-help, psychotherapy	Bias based on religion
Class	Negotiating Skills	Work patterns	Volunteer work	Bias based on age
Religious, philosophical, spiritual values	Decision-making process	Dysfunctions: addictions, violence, illness disabilities	Church or temple	Bias based on family status
Finances			Involvement in children's school & activities	
Autonomy skills		Social & community involvement		Bias based on disability
Affiliative skills		Ethnicity	Political action	
Education & work				
Social participation				

Models of Human Behavior in the Social Environment

The nine dimensions all have a direct and indirect effect upon human behavior. Moreover, people, environment, and time interweave with each other continuously. Relationships are reconfigured as multiple influences on human behavior ebb and flow. The actions of one person can only be understood in relation to the actions of other people and in relation to ever-changing situations. A focus on changing relationships among inseparable aspects of a unity is often referred to as a transactional approach (Altman & Rogoff, 1987; Dewey & Bentley, 1949). A basic tenet is that a person and their environment depend on each other for their definition; the same person in a different environment, or the same environment with a different person will most likely yield different behaviors. In reality, of course, any configuration or situation involves multiple persons and multiple environments.

Thinking about environment in multidimensional terms has proved beneficial to social workers, making it easier to understand how clients can respond to various new environments. This is essential when deciphering intervention processes and techniques.

However, gaining a global view of the framework of the model of human behavior is necessary to be an effective social worker. There are certain fundamental assumptions that make up an entire social system. Let's review the five major fundamental assumptions.

1) THE WHOLE SYSTEM IS DIFFERENT FROM THE SUM OF ITS PARTS: IT HAS DEFINITE PROPERTIES OF ITS OWN (ANDERSON & CARTER, 1990).

Each social system has an identity of its own that is different from the identities of its individual members. It is the way in which individual members relate to one another, how they organize themselves to work together toward their common purpose, which gives the social system its unique identity. For example, two hospitals may serve the same patient population, employ the same type and number of staff, and share the same mission. Despite these similarities in composition, each may have distinctly different reputations with regard to quality and medical outcomes of care. Many factors, including distribution of power, patterns of organization and communication, degrees of involvement with the community, etc., may effectively form two distinct institutional cultures. Simply put, when the component parts of systems are combined, they take on characteristics that they did not possess in isolation. In order to be effective, social workers must acknowledge and respect this wholeness, whether examining an individual, a family, an organization or the broader.

2) ALL FORMS OF MATTER "FROM SUB-ATOMIC PARTICLES TO THE ENTIRE UNIVERSE" CAN BE VIEWED AS SYSTEMS, AND ALL SYSTEMS HAVE CERTAIN COMMON PROPERTIES THAT CAUSE THEM TO BEHAVE ACCORDING TO A COMMON SET OF "RULES" (ANDERSON & CARTER, 1990).

This is a basic assumption of a social systems approach, and one that makes generalist practice possible. This is the principle that allows us to view a school system as a client as easily as we see an individual person as such. If both function as systems, then both share common characteristics, both will behave in certain predictable ways, and both will potentially be responsive to social work intervention. This statement, of course, oversimplifies the issues for the sake of explanation, but it is nonetheless effective. As noted by Berger and Federico: The physical and social sciences share the belief that the universe has some underlying order and that behavior, be it the behavior of atomic particles or interacting individuals, is a patterned, regulated activity than can be understood and, in many instances, predicted and controlled (Berger & Federico, 1982).

3) A CHANGE IN ONE PART OF A SYSTEM OR IN THE RELATIONSHIP BETWEEN PARTS WILL CREATE CHANGE IN THE SYSTEM AS A WHOLE.

Because systems are composed of interrelated parts that operate in transaction with one another, "whatever affects one part of the system affects all parts to some degree"(Hollis, 1972,p. 11).

4) EVERY SYSTEM MUST BE ABLE TO ADAPT TO CHANGING INTERNAL AND EXTERNAL DEMANDS AND CHALLENGES WHILE CONTINUING TO MAINTAIN ITS IDENTITY AND ITS UNIQUE SENSE OF WHOLENESS. SOME DEGREE OF STRESS AND TENSION IS THEREFORE A NATURAL AND, INDEED, NECESSARY PART OF ANY ADAPTIVE SYSTEM'S EXISTENCE AS IT INTERACTS WITH ITS ENVIRONMENT AND DEVELOPS OVER TIME.

As noted previously, all systems are goal-oriented or purpose-driven. That is, the system's components, or subsystems, work together to achieve common goals. When the system's components are able to work together effectively, the system is said to be "functional" or "adaptive." In other words, a functional system is one in which:

- ❖ The system is flexible enough to change as necessary in response to constantly changing conditions and demands from within and from the environment.
- ❖ While remaining flexible, the system is cohesive enough to maintain its sense of "wholeness." The subsystems are able to fulfill their individual needs and purposes while working together successfully fulfill the overall system's goals over time.
- ❖ The system works to maintain a "good fit" with its environment, and as the system develops, it becomes increasingly capable of responding to change and improving its system–environment "fit."

Obviously, the reverse is true for dysfunctional or maladaptive systems. Here, the system's components are less successful in working together to achieve the system's goals. Such a system may be so internally disorganized that its components are unable to work together effectively. On the other hand, the system may be rigid and inflexible, and therefore less able to adjust to changing circumstances and demands. Over time, such a system will be less and less likely to develop the capacities required to respond to changing circumstances while maintaining effective functioning.

5) EVERY SYSTEM IS AT THE SAME TIME A UNIT UNTO ITSELF, MADE UP OF INTERACTING PARTS, AND A PART OF A LARGER WHOLE.

Anderson and Carter (1990) borrow the term holon (Arthur Koestler,1967) to describe this phenomenon: Each entity is simultaneously a part and a whole. The unit is made up of parts to which it is the whole, the suprasystem, and at the same time, is a part of some larger whole of which it is a component or subsystem. The individual human being is a whole system composed essentially of three subsystems that interact to promote the individual's development through life: the biological system (the physical body), the psychological system (thoughts, feelings, and behaviors) and the sociocultural environmental system (the social and physical environments). On the other hand, the individual human being is itself a subsystem (i.e., component part) of a suprasystem (a larger system); that is, the family. As a family member (subsystem of the family), the individual works with other family members (other subsystems) to maintain family functioning. These examples, which are again simplified for the sake of understanding, can be extended, ad infinitum, with the family seen as a subsystem of a community, the community as a subsystem of a nation or larger culture, and a nation as a subsystem of a global community.

Diversity

As globalization and equality of human rights sweep the globe, the concept of diversity will continue to grow in importance. Consequently, diversification laws in socio-economic, religious, gender, culture, and sexual orientation will endure. As a social worker, it is important to recognize diversity and respect laws that govern equality. Discrimination laws in the U.S. protect genders, religious choice, workers' wages and many other established rights.

Effects of the Environment on Client System Behavior

The client system has changed dramatically during the 20th century. As the 1960s unfolded, a reform approach began to take hold as calls for more outreach programs and more serious study of specific social forces and the nature of their influence became louder. Sociological models, particularly those related to ethnicity, social class, and social roles, became increasingly prevalent into social work literature. The interests of various minority groups led to the War on Poverty, the Civil Rights Movement, and the Women's and Gay Liberation movements. All of these had significant roles in shaping the practice of modern social work. Due to the rapid increase in the recognition of various groups, it became increasingly difficult to categorize these entities. This gave birth to stereotyping.

Stereotyping is a public belief about certain social groups or types of individuals. Many times the concepts of stereotyping and prejudice are confused with other meanings. Stereotypes are standardized conceptions of groups based on prior assumptions. Why does this often happen?

The major source characteristics are expertise, trustworthiness, and interpersonal attraction or attractiveness. A key variable here is credibility. If a

17

famous or authoritative person sends a message, one is more apt to believe them.

Although stereotyping has gained a negative connotation, the theory does help to expedite the categorization of the complexities of people. By observing the general characteristics of a particular class or group of people, in theory, stereotyping saves time to predict a social environment.

Assessment

Social History and Collateral Data

Social work has long identified human behavior as an interaction of person with environment. Working with people within their environment is at the heart of the social work profession's approach to helping communities. This perspective underscores "the interdependence of individuals within their families, other social networks, communities and larger environments" (Northern & Kurland, 2001, p. 49). From its inception, the profession has drawn from a variety of disciplines (for example, psychology, sociology, biology, anthropology, economics, and political science) to inform its theoretical base for practice. Over time, it has attempted (with greater or lesser degrees of success) to synthesize data from these disparate fields to develop a theory base and practice models that reflect its traditional dual focus: to enhance the biopsychosocial functioning of individuals and families and to improve societal conditions (Greene, 1991).

Problem Identification

For social work assessments that are clear and directly related to the real-world problems that clients present, case theory provides a means of conceptualizing assessment and formulating assessments that are not only accurate and in- formative but also lead directly to relevant interventions. Case theory provides a set of ideas to understand and treat the symptoms or problems in functioning of one particular client (client may refer to an individual, family, group, community, or organization).

Assessment of Client System's Strengths and Challenges

Although the client system has proven itself an effective tool in assisting disadvantaged members of the community, it is always evolving. As our human environment changes, so do the needs of the community. Furthermore, a client's past and present cognitive, biological, and emotional functions are inseparable. Thus, multiple arrangements for assistance are often required to help each individual. Getting various agencies to work seamlessly is an expensive and arduous process in an ever-evolving society.

Assessment of Addictive Behaviors

Behaviorism can be studied in a systematic and observable manner without the need for internal mental states. Two major types of conditioning are classical and operant. Classical utilizes a naturally occurring stimulus paired with a response, while operant is the method of learning through rewards and punishments.

Behaviorism is more concerned with behavior than with thinking, feeling, or knowing. It focuses on the objective and observable components of behavior. The behaviorist theories all share some version of stimulus-response mechanisms for learning. Behaviorism originated with the work of John B. Watson, an American psychologist. Watson held the view that psychology should only concern itself with the study of behavior, and he was not concerned with the mind or with human consciousness. He considered it paramount that men could be studied objectively, like rats and apes. Watson's work was based on the experiments of Ivan Pavlov, and classical conditioning.

Nowadays, behaviorism is associated with the name of B.F. Skinner, who made his reputation by testing Watson's theories in the laboratory. Skinner ultimately rejected Watson's almost exclusive emphasis on reflexes and conditioning. Skinner believed that people respond to their environment, but they also operate on the environment to produce certain consequences. Thus, they participate in a feedback loop as an important part of a larger system.

Skinner developed the theory of "operant conditioning," the idea that we behave the way we do because this kind of behavior has had certain consequences in the past.

Presuppositions of behaviorism:

- ❖ Behaviorism is naturalistic. This means that the material world is the ultimate reality, and everything can be explained in terms of natural laws. Man has no soul and no mind, only a brain that responds to external stimuli.

- ❖ A central tenet of behaviorism is that thoughts, feelings, intentions, and mental processes do not determine what we do. Behaviorism views behavior as the product of conditioning. Humans are biological machines and do not consciously act; rather, they react to stimuli.

- ❖ Behaviorism teaches that we are not responsible for our actions. If we are mere machines, without minds or souls, reacting to stimuli and operating on our environment to attain certain ends, then anything we do is inevitable.

- ❖ Behaviorism is manipulative. It seeks not merely to understand human behavior, but to predict and control it. From his theories, Skinner developed the idea of "shaping." By controlling rewards and punishments, you can shape the behavior of another person.

There are several strategies to help individuals with addictive behaviors. One of the most prominent used in social work is the Transtheoretical Model (refer to Figure 1). The model has stages that reflect the thought process of clients dealing with addictive behaviors. Using this model, social workers can effectively help clients to recognize the consequences and the impact their behaviors have on others. Additionally, they can use a method called the readiness ruler to help assess the client's readiness to change when the client is in the precontemplative stage.

One behavior that social workers must be cognizant of is defensive functioning, an ego function often found in direct practice. Defensive functioning is an unconscious attempt to protect oneself from an identity-threatening feeling. This behavior is initially developed during infancy.

This form of conditioning is an approach to mental health treatment that uses the principles of behavior modification in making improvements to behavior or inner experience. The method relies on a person's ability to use imagery for purposes such as mental rehearsal. In some populations, it has been found that an imaginary reward can be as effective as a real one.

People with dependent personality disorder often want to please their providers, so they may appear cooperative and compliant on the surface. They are likely to seek frequent reassurance and may be in danger of becoming dependent on the social worker to meet their need for approval and attention. When developing a therapeutic relationship, it is important to set healthy boundaries and keep in mind that the client may feel a strong desire to gain positive reinforcement. Clients with dependent personality disorder typically need approval and reassurance, so they often try to appear cooperative to please the social worker. People with dependent personality are often easy to establish a rapport with, as they tend to try to please the social worker. They are less likely to drop out of treatment than people with other disorders. People with dependent personality disorder do not necessarily lack social skills, nor do they lack the ability to express basic emotions. This is more typical of schizoid personality disorder. A dramatic presentation is more characteristic of histrionic personality disorder than dependent personality disorder.

Behavior therapy can be used to treat many psychological conditions such as depression, ADD, ADHD, obsessive-compulsive disorder, and specific addictions. Information is obtained from the patient to identify the behaviors that cause stress, reduce quality of life, and have a negative impact. Training goals include desensitization, environmental modifications, and relaxation.

Schizophrenia tends to cause other conditions such as anxiety disorders and major depression. Substance abuse is at 40% with social problems that lead to poverty, unemployment and homelessness. The average life expectancy of individuals with schizophrenia is 10 to 12 years less than fpr those without the disorder.

Assessment of Mental & Behavioral Disorders

Behavioral disorders are manifested in several ways. Often, individuals use certain behaviors in an attempt to resolve negative experiences. If left unchecked, such behavioral disorders could become permanent fixtures in a person's life. Instead of facilitating the behavior, studies show that it is best to implement positive activities that help individuals to overcome the behavior.

Client assessments will often reveal key details about how to approach treatment with the client. For instance, clients with dependent personality disorder typically need approval and reassurance, so they often try to appear cooperative to please the social worker. The client may be superficially compliant with treatment to try gain approval, but may struggle to make lasting change.

Part of social workers' duties include recommending therapeutic treatments for various disorders. Several therapies exist, but most fall into four categories, namely, cognitive, addictions, behavioral, and anxiety. During these treatments, a social worker will be able to analyze the information gathered from the patient and make temporary changes in their daily activities.

The way people react when protecting their identity-threatened feelings is called defensive functioning. As one grows up, they develop more sophisticated styles of defenses. Most adults have advanced ways of dealing with reality and various anxieties.

Autism spectrum disorder (ASD) is a range of complex neurodevelopment disorders, characterized by social impairments, communication difficulties, and restricted, repetitive, and stereotyped patterns of behavior. Autistic disorder, sometimes called autism or classical ASD, is the most severe form of ASD, while other conditions along the spectrum include a milder form known as Asperger's Syndrome, childhood disintegrative disorder and pervasive developmental disorder not otherwise specified (usually referred to as PDD-NOS). Although ASD varies significantly in character and severity, it occurs in all ethnic and socioeconomic groups and affects every age group. Experts estimate that 1 out of 88 children age 8 will have an ASD (Centers for Disease Control and Prevention: Morbidity and Mortality Weekly Report, March 30, 2012). Males are four times more likely to have an ASD than females.

Communication is often hindered by autism. In order to circumvent these difficulties, one can use different forms of communication. The major forms of communication are Assertive, Oral, Visual, and Sensory. Identifying how an autistic client responds to each is critical to helping them.

There is no cure for ASDs. Therapies and behavioral interventions are designed to remedy specific symptoms and can bring about substantial improvement. The ideal treatment plan coordinates therapies and interventions that meet the specific needs of individual children. Most health care professionals agree that the earlier the intervention, the better.

Educational/behavioral interventions: Therapists use highly structured and intensive skill-oriented training sessions to help children develop social and language skills, such as Applied Behavioral Analysis. Family counseling for the parents and siblings of children with an ASD often helps families cope with the particular challenges of living with a child with an ASD.

Medications: Doctors may prescribe medications for treatment of specific autism-related symptoms, such as anxiety, depression, or obsessive-compulsive disorder. Antipsychotic medications are used to treat severe behavioral problems. Seizures can be treated with one or more anticonvulsant drugs. Medication used to treat people with attention deficit disorder can be used effectively to help decrease impulsivity and hyperactivity.

Other therapies: There are a number of controversial therapies or interventions available, but few, if any, are supported by scientific studies. Parents should use caution before adopting any unproven treatments. Although dietary interventions have been helpful in some children, parents should be careful that their child's nutritional status is carefully followed.

Narcissistic Personality Disorder

The symptoms of narcissistic personality disorder are especially noticeable if the behavior emerged in childhood. Normally, negative consequences do not show themselves until adulthood. Treatment for this disorder is rarely sought and the individual blames negativities on society. Long-term insight therapy can be effective, but getting the person to commit is a problem.

Cases where the client tends to exaggerate his achievements and demonstrates an overwhelming desire for success, power, and love are prominent signs of narcissistic personality disorder. Those suffering with this disorder believe they are only understood by other who reign superior in some aspect of life.

Other Behavioral Disorders

Children and young adult clients sometime display various behavioral disorders. Some that are prominent are antisocial personality disorder, bipolar disorder, ADHD, and compulsive behavior disorder. Another disorder among children and adolescents is oppositional defiant disorder. Caseworkers should be cognizant of the prominent symptoms of ODD—strongly active defiance with adult requests and excessive arguing.

Oppositional defiant disorder is an ongoing pattern of uncooperative, hostile, and defiant behavior towards authority figures. The symptoms are mostly noticed at home and school, with 16% of students suffering from this disorder. Talking back, questioning rules, and resentment are just a few of the demonstrated signs. Symptoms of oppositional defiant disorder include excessive arguing, easily annoyed by others, hateful when talking, active defiance with adult requests, and frequent temper tantrums. Oppositional defiant disorder describes children with serious behaviors that are uncooperative and hostile towards authority figures. The problem is often observed at home and school, affecting a child's family, social, and academic life.

Impulse Control Disorder and Anti-Social Personality Disorder

Impulse control is the ability to manage aggressive wishes without immediate action through behavior. Problems with this ego function are common. Many individuals who suffer with this problem display sexual promiscuity, binge eating, and excessive drug or alcohol use.

People with an impulse control disorder can't resist the urge to do something harmful to themselves or others. Impulse control disorders include addictions to alcohol or drugs, eating disorders, compulsive gambling, paraphilias, sexual fantasies and behaviors involving non-human objects, suffering, humiliation of children, compulsive hair pulling, stealing, fire setting and intermittent explosive attacks of rage.

Anti-social personality disorder is a pattern of disregard for and violations of the rights of others. It begins in childhood and progresses on until adulthood. Individuals with this disorder display poor behavioral controls such as annoyance, aggression, irritability, and verbal abuse.

Anxiety and Avoidant Personality Disorder

Anxiety is described as a response to complications that affect our everyday lives. Examples would be a pending divorce, losing a job, or a child failing school. These are considered psychological triggers that motivate us to try and resolve the problem. Anxiety disorders are cultivated by an individual's responses to minor and reoccurring problems. When the person feels as though the problem will not end and it disrupts ones about o problem solve, an anxiety disorder is apparent. The five major classes of anxiety disorders are: Generalized Anxiety Disorder, Social Phobia (Social Anxiety Disorder), Post-Traumatic Stress Disorders (PTSD), Obsessive-Compulsive Disorder, and Panic Disorder.

People who suffer from Avoidant Personality Disorder, as apparent with the pattern of social inhibition, feelings of inadequacy, sensitivity to negative evaluation, and avoidance of social interaction. People with this disorder consider themselves to be personally unappealing and fear being ridiculed, humiliated, or rejected. Avoidant Personality Disorder is first recognized in early childhood and associated with rejection by peers or parents.

Withdrawal from Addictive Substances

When people decrease or stop using substances, they will experience withdrawal symptoms if they were dependent on those substances. Withdrawal symptoms can be dangerous, but unless there's an obvious medical emergency, it is up to the client to determine if he wants to seek medical attention. Although withdrawal can become life-threatening, the client is not exhibiting any signs of a medical emergency, so the social worker cannot break the client's confidentiality. Unless there's a medical emergency, the proper course is to explain the possible risks to the client and discuss whether or not he wants to seek medical treatment. The tremor, the sweating, and the vomiting could be symptoms of a serious medical issue, so it could be dangerous simply to encourage the client to tough it out. The client may interpret this advice as encouragement to drink, which may cause more problems for him.

Dynamics and Indicators of Abuse and Neglect

As seen with the above text, abuse and neglect come in varied forms. Identifying the dynamics of these is essential to social work. However, after identifying abuse or neglect a decision must be made. When one notice these traits, first a proper assessment of the situation as a whole must take place. Is there a medical emergency present? If not, it is best to talk to the client about the possible dangers of withdrawal and allow the client to make their own decision about whether or not to seek medical help. Unless there is a medical emergency, the proper course is to explain the possible risks to the client and discuss whether or not they want to seek medical treatment.

Direct and Indirect Practice

Direct practice in social work constitutes one-on-one contact with people at the micro level and is usually identified as working with people directly at the individual, group, or family level. Rather than specifying a particular theory, direct practice is seen as an eclectic process, structured by the problem-solving process with the guiding underlying principles of sensitivity to social diversity and promotion of social and economic justice. At the micro-level, this most often involves bringing services to and improving the quality of life of people who are vulnerable and oppressed. However, direct practitioners must also be able to assess different systems levels beyond the individual and determine the appropriate intervention and its appropriate level (micro, meso, and macro), and to know when and how to implement various theories. This complex undertaking is not taught in a systematic way but rather is guided by the development of personal awareness, knowledge of social work values and ethics, sensitivity to social diversity, and promotion of social justice.

Indicators and Effects of Crisis and Change

Crisis situations are sometimes obvious, yet at other times they may be hidden. This is especially the case when dealing with physical or substance abuse and suicide. For instance, with suicide one may be quite verbal with their feelings. Others may not. Treatments given in a hospitalization may actually give a client the energy to complete a suicide. Hence, it is essential that a caseworker recognize the indicators of a crisis.

Intervention Processes and Techniques

When establishing treatment goals, it is important to teach people skills that they can use during and after treatment. Sometimes solving the current problem will not give them these skills. Teaching people new skills and how to apply them to their lives can assist them in making progress after treatment ends. In couples therapy, sometimes each person wants their spouse to be "fixed." It is important to keep longer-term goals in mind while helping the couple with their immediate marital issues. It is correct to help them learn new skills that they can use to address the problem of disagreements over chores as well as other problems in their relationship. Working on goals individually may not help the clients improve their communication or conflict resolution as a couple. Addressing the issue of household responsibilities may be helpful, but teaching them skills they can use after treatment ends is likely to be more beneficial. Although sometimes people require individual therapy before they can make progress in couples therapy – especially if there are serious mental health issues – this does not appear necessary in this case.

Self-help methods make up another technique style that can aid clients to recover from various conditions and behaviors. One that is slowly rising in popularity is covert conditioning. This therapy style uses the mind's ability to spontaneously generate imagery that can provide intuitive solutions or even improve an individual's typical reaction to situations. Imaginary rewarding has been found to be most effective in this therapy.

Humanistic therapy overlaps considerably with existential approaches and emphasizes the growth and fulfillment of the self through self-mastery, self-examination, and creative expression. Although the influences of the unconscious and society are taken into account, freedom of choice in creating one's experience is at the core.

Empathy is the appreciation of a client's situation from the client's point of view. The therapist must demonstrate emotional understanding and sensitivity to the client's feelings. One way to convey empathy is by actively listening and paying attention to what the client is saying.

Cognitive therapy is a form of direct practice that involves helping clients develop skills in identifying distorted thinking, modifying beliefs, changing behaviors, and relating to others in different ways. Difficulties are overcome by identifying and changing emotional responses, behaviors, and dysfunctional thinking.

Behavior therapy begins with the analysis of a trained therapist. The therapist analyzes the behaviors of a patient that cause stress, reduce the client's quality of life, or have a negative impact. Once this analysis is complete, the therapist chooses an appropriate treatment technique.

Person-centered therapy was developed by Carl Rogers. This type of therapy diverged from the traditional views of the therapist as an expert and moved instead toward a non-directive approach that embodied the theory of actualizing tendency. The theory of actualizing tendency says humans have the potential to discover the realization of their own personal abilities. The foundation of this method of therapy is derived from the belief that every human being strives to find their own fulfillment and the fulfillment of his or her own potential. Carl R. Rogers stated that, "Individuals have within themselves vast resources for self-understanding and for altering their self-concepts, basic attitudes, and self-directed behavior; these resources can be tapped if a definable climate of facilitative psychological attitudes can be provided".

Cognitive therapy is a comprehensive system of psychotherapy, and treatment is based on an elaborated and empirically supported theory of psychopathology and personality. It has been found to be effective in more than 400 outcome studies for a myriad of psychiatric disorders, including depression, anxiety disorders, eating disorders, and substance abuse, among others, and it is currently being tested for personality disorders. It has also been demonstrated

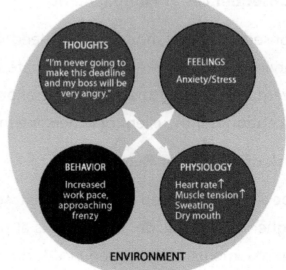

to be effective as an adjunctive treatment to medication for serious mental disorders such as bipolar disorder and schizophrenia. Cognitive therapy has been extended to and studied for adolescents and children, couples, and families. Its efficacy has also been established in the treatment of certain medical disorders, such as irritable bowel syndrome, chronic fatigue syndrome, hypertension, fibromyalgia, post-myocardial infarction depression, noncardiac chest pain, cancer, diabetes, migraine, and other chronic pain disorders.

Developed by Aaron T. Beck, MD, in the mid-1960s, cognitive therapy is a short-term, structured therapy that uses an information-processing model to understand and treat psychopathological conditions. The theory is based, in part, on a phenomenological approach to psychology, as proposed by Epictetus and other Greek Stoic philosophers and more contemporary theorists such as Adler, Alexander, Horney, and Sullivan. The approach emphasizes the role of individuals' views of themselves and their personal worlds as being central to their behavioral reactions, as espoused by Kelly, Arnold, and Lazarus. Cognitive therapy was also influenced by theorists such as Ellis, Bandura, Lewinsohn, Mahoney, and Meichenbaum.

Consequences of Nonpayment

Consequences of nonpayment need to be addressed prior to ending any services. Social workers may terminate services to a client that is not paying an overdue balance if the contract arrangements have been made clear. The only exception is if the client or others are in imminent danger.

Risk of Suicide or Relapse

Social workers need to know what sorts of factors may place clients at a higher risk for suicide. This client is at particular risk due to depression and the improvements they experienced during hospitalization. When people are feeling better, they sometimes find the energy to plan and follow through with suicide. There's no reason to believe that the hours people work put them at higher risk for suicide. Caucasians are at a higher risk than other groups. There's no evidence that having adult children who have moved out of the home puts clients at a higher risk.

When clients are precontemplative, they can often benefit from interventions that help them assess the pros and cons of their behaviors and their willingness and readiness to change. Motivational interviewing is an excellent strategy to help clients who are precontemplative. Clients in the action stage should be already changing behaviors to help them live a healthier lifestyle. When a client is in the maintenance stage, they have already recognized the impact of their behavior and are trying to maintain changes. Clients in the preparation stage should be taking steps to help them begin making the changes. All these strategies are most likely to be effective with a client who is precontemplative.

Neglected Children

Children who have experienced neglect sometimes hoard food, even when they are placed in foster or adoptive homes. They have learned this as a survival skill and should not be punished. Instead, they should be given support. Caregivers can help them learn to recognize that their needs will be taken care of. Over time, with helpful reinforcement, these behaviors are likely to diminish. Punishing the child is not likely to be effective and may have the opposite effect, as it will likely increase his anxiety. Locking the food up will likely cause increased anxiety for the child as he will not have access to food, which is the fear that is driving his behavior. Ignoring is only a good tactic if the child is exhibiting attention-seeking behaviors.

Self-Determination

A core principle of social work is the client's right to self-determination. The NASW Code of Ethics is clear that social workers should support a client's right to self-determination, unless a client is posing a risk to self or someone else. Social workers should set aside their own values and encourage clients to make their own choices based on what they think is right for them. Although it may be appropriate at times to discuss the pros and cons of a decision, clients need to know that ultimately the decision is up to them. Telling the client to look at how their actions will be viewed by Child Protective Services may put pressure on the client and may make the social worker's values about it known. It may or may not be true that children would benefit from the client's efforts to regain custody. The social worker should not try to persuade the client one way or the other. It is appropriate to tell the client that they have the right to choose how to respond to child protective services. Insisting the client work to regain custody does not support the client's right to self-determination.

Matching Intervention with Client System Needs

One prominent skill and intervention technique is persuasion. Persuasion induces a change of attitude through communication. Yale psychologist Carl Hovland states that there are factors that can affect the persuasiveness of a message. These factors are known as Source, Message, and Audience.

Administrators should secure proper training for social workers to respond in a case of emergency. Professional services need to be provided to the greatest extent possible. Victims may require help with trauma, loss of housing, or loss of a loved one.

Documentation

Macro communication is utilized in social work practice on a regular basis and consists of words in written or oral formats. There are four different types used in policy, advocacy, management, and practice. They include fiduciary, task, public relations, and persuasion.

Interviewing

Interviewing is a prominent part of a social worker's job. In this initial phase of interaction with the client, one should be able to assess issues, needs, and the background of the client. At times, sensitive information will be discussed and it is necessary for social workers to understand how to engage and reply in these circumstances. Non-judgmental questions can effectively encourage discussion about sensitive subjects such as abuse, neglect, sexuality, and suicide

Evidence-Based Practice

Theories within social work practice are beneficial; however, evidence-based practice (EBP) has certain advantages over the former. By using the best evidence available, caseworkers can analyze a case on actual evidence instead of theorizing. This can be helpful in communication, intervention, and other direct and indirect practice areas.

For instance, in the realm of communication, caseworkers can effectively use macro communication to help community planners form better working relationships with community members. Based on the evident needs of the community and the expertise of the community planner, a caseworker is able to dismiss theory for actual evidence.

Professional Relationships, Values, and Ethics

Ethical responsibility to the client system and profession

As a professional, there are certain responsibilities and ethics that you must uphold. These foster fairness and honor to the client system and social work profession. Technology used in the wrong way could hinder one's ability to uphold their ethical responsibilities. You must render caution when considering the use of electronic media, and discuss with each client the potential risks, benefits, and consequences of receiving services via electronic media.

Social workers play an integral role during times of local or national emergencies. Since many clients rely upon social workers for support, it is best that social workers provide it to the best of their ability. In this way, social workers can serve as a mediator in communicating and helping client to respond to city or national authorities.

Confidentiality

Every client has the right to confidentiality. However, the life and safety of the client take precedence over confidentiality. Therefore, a caseworker must recognize how to handle specific situations to ensure confidentiality is respected while caring for the client's safety. This is especially the case when working cases involving minors. Even in situations where adults like parents, teachers, and others have limited authority over the minor's life, confidentiality must be upheld when there is no danger to the client's life. Caseworkers can talk to clients about whether or not they would want any information disclosed and convey the possible implications of disclosing information.

Care also must be taken when openly discussing the details of any client case. Caseworkers can be held responsible for conversations overheard in non-controlled areas. Even in cases where caseworkers know the clients personally or know relatives of the clients, they must refrain from sharing confidential information. When conducting various evaluations and participant research studies, caseworkers should obtain consent form the participant and protect client anonymity.

Adolescents have a right to confidentiality. Unless the adolescent poses a risk to self or others, the information the client discloses should be protected. Even when there is a release of information in place, disclosure should be on a need-to-know basis, and the client should participate in any discussion about whether or not to disclose the information. Although the guardian signed the release of information, this does not imply the social worker must release all the information to everyone. The client should be consulted about what information she wants released. It is appropriate to discuss with the client whether or not they want others to be informed, and they should be warned of the possible implications. A supervisor does not need to be consulted, as it is up to the client if they wants the information released. The client has a right to privacy and others do not need to know the client's current issues.

Social workers are obligated by the NASW Code of Ethics to respect confidentiality and ensure that colleagues understand that, also. Outside influences should not dictate loose communication of disclosed client information. The social work administrator needs to stress the importance of private information in regards to other professional relationships.

Electronic Media

The NASW states that social workers should use caution when providing services via electronic media. Social workers should ensure that clients are aware of the potential risks as well as benefits so they can make an informed decision about whether or not they wish to have this service. It is important to discuss the risks and potential consequences with clients so that clients are aware how services delivered via electronic media differ from face-to-face contact. Whether or not the social worker can provide electronic services does not depend on whether they are already receiving these services with a doctor. Social workers can provide these services when caution used. It is possible to establish a therapeutic relationship with clients even if they are not face to face with the social worker.

Confidentiality in Evaluation and Research

Social workers engaged in evaluation and research techniques should protect the anonymity and confidentiality of their participants. Limits of confidentiality and the measures that will be taken to destroy data records after proper usage must be discussed with the client. All identifying information should be omitted unless proper consent has been given.

Asking about Sexual Orientation

When addressing issues about sexual preference, ask questions in a non-judgmental fashion and make it clear what information you are looking for. During an assessment, this closed-question approach can help put clients at ease and encourage them to answer clearly and succinctly. This question, asked in a non-judgmental fashion, is the most effective way to encourage a discussion of sexual preference. Clients may be uncertain about what information to provide, and may not be clear what you mean when you use the words sexual preference. Often, people do not think of themselves as falling into a category of gay or straight – for many, sexuality is fluid or they eschew labels or political identification, and may not know how to answer a close-ended question such as "Are you gay or straight?" Use open-ended questions instead, such as "Do you prefer sex with men, women, or both?"

Religious Discrimination

Religious discrimination is the adverse work treatment of employees based on their on their religious beliefs or practices rather than on the employee's merit. The Civil Rights Act of 1964 prohibits religious discrimination in the manner of hiring, firing, and other conditions of employment. Reasonable accommodations include flexible paid holidays, schedules, PTO for religious observances, and the right to wear religion-required head gear.

Social Equality

Social equality includes equal rights such as freedom of speech, security, property rights, and access to health care. It involves equal opportunities that include society as a whole. Gender, origin, age, sexual orientation, income, language, and disability must not result in unequal treatment under the law or reduce opportunities. Social equality makes reference to social rather than income or economic equality.

Client's right to self-determination

Self-determination is a given right that must be respected in the social work profession. Ethical protocol demands that caseworkers allow clients to choose how to respond to various situations and services.

Methods of Professional Development

Professional development within the social work industry is ongoing. Occasionally, it will be necessary to acquire additional training to work in certain fields. For instance, hospitals, psychiatric facilities, and other specialty agencies may offer or mandate continuous training to improve one's competency. These can come in the form of conferences and seminars that aim to increase a social worker's expertise and competency.

Communicating effectively with management is vital to social work. Task communication in the industry facilitates three major purposes:

(1) to ensure the delivery of a quality product or service

(2) to establish a co-operative, competent workforce

(3) to provide corrective feedback. Effective task communication is an excellent way to initiate public hearings.

Public hearings that are informational, seek citizen input, and are deliberative are successful avenues of communication in management practice. Another good source is surveys. These communicate the needs and resources of a community.

Administrators need to stress the importance of social workers only accepting work based on the willingness to acquire the necessary competency. All supervisees should strive to become proficient in their performance of professional practice. The administrator needs to mandate attendance at trainings to ensure social workers stay current with emerging knowledge relevant to their need of knowledge.

Practice Exam

1) A family has adopted a seven-year-old boy who had previously experienced severe neglect. The adoptive parents are meeting with a social worker because they are frustrated that he continues to hoard food. They report that they often find food under his bed and he "steals" extra food to put in his backpack for school. What recommendations should the social worker make?

    A. The parents should take away privileges each time they discover that he is hoarding food.

    B. They should install locks on the cupboards and the refrigerator so they can better monitor his food intake.

    C. The parents should ignore the behavior, as it will likely go away on its own once the child realizes that the family has plenty of food.

    D. They can provide the child with a food basket where he can keep his healthy snacks and they can refill the basket when it is nearing empty.

---

2) A social worker is employed at a doctor's office. The program director, who is a doctor at the office, reports that the office will begin providing services via video conferencing to established clients who live in rural areas. The purpose is to increase access to services for clients who lack reliable transportation. What should the social worker do?

    A. Discuss with each client the potential risks, benefits, and consequences of receiving services via electronic media.

    B. Begin services with clients who have already begun receiving service via video conferencing with a doctor.

    C. Inform the program manager that social workers are not allowed to provide telemedicine.

    D. Explain to the program manager that social workers cannot establish therapeutic relationships with clients when clients are not physically present.

3) A 57-year-old male has been meeting with a social worker to address his alcohol dependence. Over the past few weeks, he has cut down on his drinking. His arrives at his scheduled appointment sweating. He states he has been vomiting and he has a noticeable tremor in his hands. How should the social worker respond?

    A. Call 911, even if the client refuses to consent, as the client is likely detoxing and may experience seizures or possibly death.

    B. Talk to the client about the possible dangers of alcohol withdrawal and allow the client to make his own decision about whether or not to seek medical help.

    C. Encourage the client to withstand the uncomfortable symptoms for a few days as they will likely pass after the painful process of detox.

    D. Encourage the client to decrease his alcohol intake more slowly as he is less likely to suffer such serious withdrawal symptoms.

---

4) A social worker is meeting with a 50-year-old African-American male who acknowledges he has some suicidal ideation. He was previously diagnosed with major depression and was recently discharged from an inpatient hospitalization. He reports that following his hospitalization he has more energy and feels better. He lives at home with his wife and his adult children have moved out of the home. He works in construction and states that he works about 60 hours per week. What suicide risk factors should the social worker pay close attention to?

    A. The long hours that he works put him at a higher risk of suicide.

    B. The client is African-American and therefore, statistically, a higher suicide risk.

    C. Having adult children who have moved out of the home puts him at a higher risk.

    D. His improvement during his hospitalization may actually give him the energy to complete suicide.

5) A 16-year-old client is seeking services from an outpatient social worker after becoming the victim of a sexual assault. The client's mother has signed a general release of information that allows the social worker to talk to the school. The social worker receives a call from the client's math teacher who states the client's grades have declined and she wants to know if there is something "going on" with the client lately. How should the social worker respond?

    A. Contact the client's mother to determine how much information she is comfortable with the teacher knowing.

    B. Talk to the client about whether or not she would want any information disclosed and the possible implications of disclosing information.

    C. Contact a supervisor before disclosing any information.

    D. Tell the math teacher that the client was sexually assaulted.

---

6) A 32-year-old man is referred to a social worker after his children were removed by Child Protective Services due to allegations of neglect. He tells the social worker that he is not sure that he wants to fight to get them back. He states he doesn't think he wants to go through all the things child protective services wants him to do only to not regain custody in the end. Which response is the best thing the social worker should say to the client?

    A. "It's important to look at how not attempting to get custody of the children will be viewed by Child Protective Services."

    B. "Your children will benefit from knowing that you at least tried to regain custody, even if you aren't successful."

    C. "You are free to choose whether or not you want to try to regain custody of the children."

    D. "It may be helpful to work toward regaining custody initially, and if at any time you decide you want to give up, you can do so."

7) A social worker is conducting an initial assessment with a client. What is the best way for the social worker to inquire about the client's sexual orientation?

    A. "Do you prefer sex with men, women, or both?"

    B. "Tell me about your sexuality."

    C. "What is your sexual preference?"

    D. "Do you consider yourself to be gay or straight?"

---

8) A social worker has started to treat a woman who has been diagnosed with dependent personality disorder. The woman reports a variety of failed relationships. She acknowledges that she often makes unhealthy choices in the kinds of partners that she picks. When establishing a therapeutic relationship with the client, what sort of information should the social worker keep in mind?

    A. The client may be superficially compliant with treatment and to try gain approval but may struggle to make lasting change.

    B. Establishing rapport will be difficult and the client is likely to drop out of treatment early.

    C. The client is likely to have difficulty expressing her emotions and most likely lacks basic social skills.

    D. The client's dramatic presentation and desire to be the center of attention may interfere with developing the therapeutic relationship.

9) A social worker is working on values clarification with a client who has a dependence on alcohol. The social worker is also assisting the client in recognizing the consequences and the impact his behaviors have on others. The social worker uses a readiness ruler to help assess the client's readiness to change. These methods are most likely to be effective when the client is in which stage of the Transtheoretical Model?

    A. Action

    B. Maintenance

    C. Preparation

    D. Precontemplation

---

10) A couple requests help in improving their seven-year marriage. When you ask them about their goals, they begin to argue almost immediately. The husband states his wife nags him too much about chores. The wife states her husband is lazy. How should you proceed with establishing treatment goals?

    A. Assist them in establishing treatment goals to help them learn to improve their communication and resolve conflict.

    B. Recommend that they each attend sessions with you individually to set separate goals to work on until they are ready to work together in a session.

    C. Assist them in setting a goal to help them resolve their arguments around household responsibilities.

    D. Recommend they receive individual treatment to help them work on individual issues.

11) Toby has suffered from depression his whole life. He has seen many doctors and tried several medications. The recommendation for Toby is to attend therapy that will promote positive reinforcement, social skills training, and modeling. The idea is to analyze the information gathered from the patient and make temporary changes in his daily activities. What kind of therapy should he attend?

A. Cognitive therapy

B. Addictions therapy

C. Behavior therapy

D. Anxiety therapy

12) Older teens and young adults self-report symptoms of this serious mental illness, usually before the age of 19. Contributory factors include environment, genetics, and psychological and social processes. Symptoms appear as auditory hallucinations, bizarre delusions, paranoia, and disorganized speech. This disorder mainly affects cognition, but also contributes to emotional and behavioral problems. What illness is being described?

A. Dissociative identity disorder

B. Bipolar disorder

C. Schizophrenia

D. Catatonia

13) Two colleagues are overheard discussing an abuse case in the hallway of the human service agency. One of the social workers is a relative of the client and quite concerned about what may happen. The investigating worker gives information pertaining to possible foster care placement for the children. What would an administrator see as a violation in this conversation?

A. Competency of colleagues
B. Interdisciplinary collaboration
C. Confidentiality
D. Misrepresentation

---

14) Donald is a new clinical social worker in a hospital setting. The administrator notifies him of upcoming trainings that are job-specific, but Donald denies them, stating he does not have the time. He also misses mandated conferences and seminars. When Donald is assigned a new case that becomes complicated, he is unaware of how to handle the situation. The supervisor notifies Donald that he is lacking in what area of expertise?

A. Work management
B. Competency
C. Time management
D. Professionalism

15) Rebecca is providing clinical social work in a children's hospital. One of her clients is a 4-year-old boy with autism. Communication with him has been difficult and he will not look at her when she is speaking. Rebecca notices he likes to look at the framed artwork on his hospital room wall. The social worker brings in pictures of a little boy putting on his pajamas for bed. The autistic child stares at the pictures and then pulls his own pajamas out of a drawer. Rebecca has used what form of communication?

A. Assertive

B. Oral

C. Visual

D. Sensory

16) Fred is a 16-year-old who has been in a lot of trouble. He is currently on juvenile probation for stealing property from neighbors. The adolescent will pick fights with other kids at school and within the community. Fred shows disregard for his safety and demonstrates violent behaviors. What disorder appropriately defines this teen?

A. Anti-social personality disorder

B. Manic depressive disorder

C. ADHD

D. Compulsive behavior disorder

17) Andrea accepts a position with a banking firm that promised day shift Monday through Friday. After her second month of employment, she was told Saturdays would be added to her shift every other week. Andrea explained she belonged to a church group that met every Saturday morning and she was the head teacher for their youth chapter. Her beliefs required her to be available every Saturday for worship and congregation. The banking firm refused to adhere to her requests and threatened to terminate her employment should she miss a Saturday. What form of discrimination does this describe?

A. Equal pay discrimination
B. Sex-based discrimination
C. Accommodation discrimination
D. Religious discrimination

18) Anxiety disorders develop when we have a high response to minor or common problems. Individuals who suffer with this problem feel like the anxiety never ends and it interferes with problem solving. Medication can help treat this disorder, but psychotherapy is also required. When does anxiety reach a severe problem?

A. When it interferes with problem solving
B. When thoughts turn to self-harm
C. When it alerts one to a problem
D. When it lasts for a short amount of time

19) Task communication in management practice serves three purposes: (1) to ensure the delivery of a quality product or service; (2) to establish a cooperative, competent workforce; and (3) to provide corrective feedback. What is a manner by which a social worker can make this successful?

A. Communicate through visual aides

B. Devise a discipline procedure

C. Write a letter to the local congressman

D. Initiate public hearings

20) A state of affairs in which all people within an isolated group or specific society have the same status in a certain respect is an ideal situation that rarely occurs. The argument behind this perception is cited as economics, foreign policies, and immigration. What concept is being described and requires the lack of legally enforced boundaries of unjustified discrimination motivated by a person's identity?

A. Social equality

B. Equal opportunity

C. Voting rights

D. Equal rights

21) Direct practice by a social worker may involve the ego function of defensive functioning. These develop in infancy and involve the boundary between the outer world and self. These primitive defenses include projection, denial, and splitting. What is the definition of a defense?

    A. An unconscious attempt to protect oneself from an identity-threatening feeling

    B. Conceptual thinking that may be associated with schizophrenia

    C. The capacity for mutually satisfying relationships

    D. Enables the individual to think, feel, and act in a coherent manner

---

22) Covert conditioning is often seen with self-help methods and has not reached the popularity of other therapies. Some clinicians report a mind has the ability to spontaneously generate imagery that can provide intuitive solutions or even improve an individual's typical reaction to situations. Assessing this condition, what kind of reward would be most beneficial?

    A. Money

    B. Tangible

    C. Imaginary

    D. None of the above

23) Since elementary school, Mark has demanded admiration for everything he has accomplished. He tends to exaggerate his achievements and demonstrates an overwhelming desire for success, power, and love. Mark feels he can only be understood by others like him who reign superior in some aspect of life. What disorder does this individual display?

    A. Narcissistic personality disorder

    B. Bi-polar disorder

    C. Chauvinistic personality disorder

    D. Borderline personality disorder

---

24) Oppositional defiant disorder affects 16% of school-aged children and adolescents. There are no known causes for ODD, but parents report that this problem makes children more demanding while they are young. What symptoms should appear before a social worker completes a full assessment?

    A. Active defiance with adult requests

    B. Excessive arguing

    C. Both A and B

    D. Overwhelming submissiveness

---

25) Persuasion changes attitudes in individuals and this is a response to communication. The work of Carl Hovland states there are factors that can affect the persuasiveness of a message. The target characteristic refers to the person who receives and processes the message. What is another characteristic?

    A. Self-esteem

    B. Source

    C. Attractiveness

    D. Credibility

26) People find it difficult to take in all of the complexities of others as individuals. An efficient way for many to organize blocks of information is by categorizing. This allows one to simplify, predict, and organize the world. Assigning general characteristics to a specific group of people tends to save time and predict the social environment. What does this theory reflect?

    A. Social avoidance

    B. Racial grouping

    C. Discrimination

    D. Stereotyping

27) Anna is a social worker who has been conducting evaluation and research procedures with one of her clients. She obtained consent from the individual to further knowledge in a specific area, but the client does not want her name mentioned for further purposes. Once the research is completed, Anna conducts a meeting with fellow colleagues to share her findings. What is good practice in this realm of professionalism?

    A. None of the data collected should be shared

    B. The social worker should protect the client's anonymity

    C. Obtain legal authority to give out the client's name

    D. Only mention the client's name with other professional colleagues

28) Public relations communication in community practice is aimed at establishing an appropriate working relationship between community planners and community members. An effective PR campaign must sell a vision of a planning outcome. It must respect local culture and minimize polarization of community subgroups. This is part of a format utilizing what kind of communication?

  A. Macro
  B. Aggressive
  C. Assertive
  D. Visual

29) There has been a public emergency in a small town. First responders appear to care for the injured. The social work administrator in a neighboring town calls his team of social workers in from their relaxing weekend. What is the administrator's duty?

  A. Place the social workers on call in case their services are needed
  B. Contact local service agencies to let them know the team is not available
  C. To ensure his staff provides professional services to the greatest extent possible
  D. Prepare the agency for a rush of welfare applications

30) Chris has had difficulty managing aggressive behaviors his whole life. He has been married three times and has two children who do not want to see him. Chris spent two years in jail for critically injuring a neighbor after their dog would not stop barking. What assessment would a social worker give this client?

    A. Impulse control

    B. Defensive functioning

    C. Affect regulation

    D. Judgment

31) Person-centered therapy should take place in a supportive environment created by a close personal relationship between therapist and client. The general direction of the therapy is determined by the client, while the therapist seeks to increase the client's insight and self-understanding through informal questions. Three attitudes on the part of the therapist are central to the productivity of person-centered therapy. They are congruence, unconditional positive regard, and what else?

    A. Complimentary

    B. Positive reaction

    C. Empathy

    D. Coerciveness

32) A supervisor approaches one of his workers and comments on her attire. He feels she should be able to dress a little nicer for the professional office atmosphere. The worker is a single mother who does not make much more than minimum wage. She has to pay household expenses and daycare. There is no money left over for expensive attire. The worker quits her employment and feels she is not good enough to work in that type of setting. What would be the best treatment for her through direct practice?

A. Behavior therapy
B. Cognitive therapy
C. Judgment therapy
D. Socialization therapy

33) Direct practice often utilizes behavior therapy to treat depression, ADHD, addiction, insomnia, chronic fatigue, and phobias. The length of therapeutic treatment varies with each individual client. Treatments may include assertiveness training, desensitization, and relaxation training. What is the first thing a therapist must do before beginning treatment?

A. Analyze the behaviors
B. Estimate the client's quality of life
C. Modify the environment
D. Remove undesirable behaviors

34) Autism is a spectrum disorder defined by a certain set of behaviors that children and adults exhibit in varying ways. The main symptom of autism is the abnormal or impaired development of communication and social interaction. Two people with the same diagnosis may display any combination of behaviors in any degree of severity. What criteria are needed on an assessment for an autism diagnosis?

    A. Delay in the spoken language

    B. Failure to develop peer relationships

    C. Lack of social or emotional reciprocity

    D. All of the above

---

35) A client who has been receiving counseling services by a social worker on a fee for service basis is overdue on the payments. A contract had previously been drawn up and the client agreed on the set rate. The social worker makes the decision to terminate services. Is it ethical to close a case based on nonpayment?

    A. No. The client should seek out the social worker's supervisor to rectify the problem.

    B. No. The client has a legal right to receive social work services if they cannot pay.

    C. No. The social worker should redo the payment contract to accommodate financial needs.

    D. Yes. The social worker can terminate services if there is no imminent danger to the client.

36) Five-year-old Jesse has been displaying inappropriate behaviors on the playground. He wants to take other children's toys, push them off the swings when he wants a turn, and knocks kids down to get to the slide. Jesse clearly does not like to share or wait in line during recess. His teacher started conditioning him by providing the opportunity of being first in line for recess when he displays appropriate playing behaviors the previous day. Eventually, Jesse found that he could get to the swings and slide faster if he behaved. Conditioning occurs through interaction with the environment. What theory of learning is based on the idea that all behaviors are acquired through this conditioning?

    A. Comprehension theory

    B. Behaviorism theory

    C. Anti-social theory

    D. Communication theory

37) George lives in an apartment with several tenants. He avoids all contact with his neighbors and does not have any friends. When George sees a neighbor coming down the hall, he will turn and go the other direction to evade simple conversation or eye contact. His life is very lonely and he makes no effort to rectify the situation. What kind of personality disorder does Henry suffer from?

    A. Bi-polar disorder

    B. Anti-social personality disorder

    C. Depressive disorder

    D. Avoidant personality disorder

38) Mrs. Snyder has a lot of difficulty with a student in her 4th grade class. Zachary disobeys rules, talks back, and likes to argue. He demonstrates frequent temper tantrums and will not comply with her requests. Mrs. Snyder contacts Zachary's parents for a conference and finds out the problem is also occurring at home. Recommendations are made to refer the child for what kind of evaluation?

    A. Anti-social disorder
    B. Bi-polar disorder
    C. Attention deficit hyperactivity disorder
    D. Oppositional defiant disorder

39) Cultural diversity and integrity encompasses a huge range of protections under human rights laws that include the freedom for creative activity, freedom of assembly, and freedom of religion. Cultural rights have been embodied into several human rights laws to establish diversity and respect. What law below includes cultural diversity?

    A. Convention on the Rights of the Child
    B. International Convention on the Elimination of All Forms of Racial Discrimination
    C. The International Bill of Rights
    D. All of the above

40) The humanist movement in general focuses on the idea that people are innately good and tend toward goodness. In a humanistic therapy context, there is presumption that the true nature of the human is to want to improve and reach high levels of what?

    A. Self-perception
    B. Trust
    C. Assertiveness
    D. Behavior

41) The policy of providing Permanency Planning refers to:

A. Children who are at risk of removal or are removed from their own homes

B. The development of a plan through which abused and neglected children will be assured of a stable family situation throughout childhood

C. A stable foster care plan for children removed from their homes

D. The use of adoption for children at risk

42) DSM-IV permits certain diagnoses for mental disorders to be made, even though the diagnosis does not totally fit DSM-IV criteria. These diagnoses are normally modified by the word:

A. Revised

B. Provisional

C. Temporary

D. Latent

43) A social worker and his agency supervisor are sued for malpractice by the family of a teenage boy who made several attempts at suicide and finally succeeded in killing himself. Which statement best reflects the supervisor's legal status in this lawsuit?

A. Since the supervisor was not the direct clinician and had never personally treated the youth, she is not liable for any negligent actions committed by others in the agency.

B. The supervisor shares vicarious legal liability and is responsible for carefully monitoring and evaluating the status of every case under treatment by her supervisees, and for keeping records concerning the supervisee's work on the case.

C. The agency is the only legally liable party and the workers are not individually responsible.

D. In cases such as these, parents often believe that a finding of negligence on the part of the clinician will reduce their sense of loss and failure. The lawsuit is probably frivolous and neither the worker, nor the supervisor is responsible.

---

44) A patient presents at an ambulatory care facility and is in obvious psychological distress, showing severe anxiety and paranoia. The clinician is unable to determine the exact configuration of the patient's symptoms, but is certain that it is an Anxiety Disorder. The worker is unable to determine if the is order is primary, caused by the patient's severe kidney disease or related to other factors such as the patient's continuing substance abuse. The most likely DSM-IV diagnosis is;

A. Anxiety Disorder, with generalized anxiety

B. Anxiety Disorder, undifferentiated

C. Anxiety Disorder, NOS

D. Anxiety Disorder, provisional

45) A school social worker interviews a 14-year-old female student with an IQ of 65. Though assigned to slower classes, the student maintains social relationships and is able to respond appropriately to teachers and classmates. Her schoolwork is within the range expected for her recorded IQ. She can read somewhat below grade level and is able to do very basic arithmetic. She is also able to follow instructions and is generally amiable in responding to coaching and correction.

A. In developing a plan with this student and the family, the social worker would:

B. Plan for eventual supervised residence in a facility for the mentally disabled

C. Establish a plan that includes vocational preparation and that will eventually lead to independent living.

D. Emphasize vocational achievement in the near term

---

46) After scheduling a one-hour session with at patient for an interview, you find that the hour is nearly up. However, the client begins to discuss another issue that will take additional time to consider. You have another patient scheduled shortly after this interview. The best way to proceed is to:

A. Finish the initial interview topic and schedule a different time to meet with the patient soon.

B. Allow the patient to continue, using all the time they need to explain the new issue and skip the next patient's appointment.

C. Ask the patient to give a clear rationale for why they need to talk about the new issue with you near the end of the interview.

D. Let the patient know that they have expired their scheduled hour and you have someone else to meet with.

---

47) A baby displaying drug withdrawal symptoms is set for adoptive care placement. The baby has completed a medical follow-up and you have filed the appropriate paperwork. The social worker should prepare the adopting parents by:

    A. Disclosing that the baby's biological parents had a drug addiction but ensure them that the baby will most likely not have the same problem.

    B. Disclosing that the baby has a drug background but not furnishing any further information unless asked.

    C. Never mentioning the baby's biological parent's drug background.

    D. Disclosing the baby's drug background and informing the adoptive parents about new drug treatments available; answering any inquires they might have about medical issues with the baby.

---

48) You are assigned to a clinic that specializes in alcoholism. A patient you are interviewing is obviously intoxicated. It would be most appropriate for you to:

    A. Not proceed with the interview session and inform the client that you cannot conduct an interview when he is intoxicated.

    B. Focus the entire interview on the negative consequences of alcoholism.

    C. Let the client know firmly that his case will be closed.

    D. Suggest that he seek medical assistance since your counseling is not beneficial to him.

49) While interviewing a new client that is on public assistance, the client discloses to you that he is getting as much money as he earned while working. Furthermore, the client states that it is ridiculous for anyone to work when they can get public assistance and not work. It is best to respond to this by:

    A. Refusing to talk about this with the client

    B. Strongly disagreeing with the client's statement

    C. Agreeing with the client

    D. Telling the client that this subject is dependent on each person's values

50) During an interview with a client, you find out that he recently got out of prison probation. You decide that it is necessary to contact his probation officer to gather additional information. It would be best to contact the probation officer:

    A. With the client's consent after the interview.

    B. Without the client's consent after the interview.

    C. Only if the client can be involved in the conversation.

    D. Do what you feel is best according to how the interview proceedings.

51) A client that you have worked with gave birth a few days ago. She does not want to see her newborn and is very irate with the staff. Your best course of action is to:

    A. Strongly tell the woman that she will be sent to a psychiatric facility if she does not act reasonably.

    B. Tell her that she is acting foolishly.

    C. Meet with her so you can try to assess why she is misbehaving.

    D. Tell the woman that she needs to see her child and that she will be different after she does.

52) You are assigned as a caseworker to a methadone clinic. During an interview with a client, he asks to borrow $15. If this happens, you should:

    A. Inform the client that policy prohibits you from lending money to clients.

    B. Give the client the money.

    C. Ask him to check with some of the other staff members.

    D. Tell them to ask a relative or friend.

---

53) As a social worker, you will use the questioning technique during interviews. The best reason to do so is:

    A. Discern wrong information given by the client.

    B. Show the client that they can't lie to you and get away with it.

    C. Gather the needed information to process the case.

    D. Persuade the client into a proper way of reasoning.

---

54) You have just met with a client that had a hospital stay. The patient let their boyfriend's son stay overnight at the hospital, which is contrary to hospital policy. You should:

    A. Report the patient to Child Protective Services.

    B. Privately discuss the situation with the patient to gather details of why she allowed the child to stay overnight.

    C. Meet with the patient and the boy and teach them why it was wrong to have the boy stay overnight. Explain proper parenting techniques to the woman.

    D. If the child is okay, don't do anything.

55) The best way to get a clarification of a client's statement is to:

A. Get the client to rephrase their comments.

B. Rephrase the statement yourself and ask the client is that what they meant.

C. Explain to the client that the way they are describing things makes it difficult for you to understand.

D. Assume what you believe they are saying.

56) A 12-year old enrolled at a family agency relates they are contemplating suicide. As the caseworker you are convinced that this is serious. The first thing you should do is:

A. Meet with your supervisor.

B. Send the child to a psychiatric consultant on staff.

C. Inform the child's parents or guardian after explaining to the child that you are required to do this.

D. Treat this as a part of your confidentiality requirement and keep things between you and the child.

57) One of your adult patients is nearing discharge from a local hospital and he needs to decide on a place of residence. The final decision should be made by:

A. The patient's relatives or close friends.

B. Solely by you because you are the authorized caseworker.

C. The patient and the caseworker.

D. The patient with guidance from their doctor.

58) While interviewing a child, a good caseworker uses observation techniques. This includes keeping a close eye on the child's behavior, mood, comments and feelings. This type of observation is necessary because:

A. It builds the client/caseworker relationship.

B. It helps the caseworker to ascertain vital information about the child.

C. It gives clues about when it is appropriate to humor the child.

D. It allows the caseworker to understand how the parents or guardians are treating the child.

---

59) A female client of yours has obviously been abused by her husband. She is very embarrassed and distressed, making it difficult for her to convey the details of what recently occurred. It would be best for you to:

A. Let her know that you need to know all of the details of the beating.

B. Let her know that you will leave and get back with her when she is a better state to tell her story.

C. Ask her how you can help after you tell her that you do not need to know the details of the situation right now.

D. Delay the interview until the husband can be there so that both can present their stories.

60) **An elderly man arrives at the hospital and is diagnosed with a terminal form of cancer. Unaware of the diagnosis, the man is the primary guardian of three grandchildren who were abandoned. When you ask the patient for emergency contact information so that the grandchildren can be taken care of during the patient's hospital stay, he refuses. The man states that there are no other contacts that can care for the children well.**

A. Let the children take care of themselves until the patient can decide what to do once he hears his diagnosis.

B. Tell the patient that he is dying and hat the grandchildren need to have someone care for them.

C. Explain to the patient that they will mostly likely need a short hospital stay. Next, discuss temporary options for the grandchildren and help him put together a plan.

D. Tell the patient you are calling Child Protective Services so that the grandchildren will be taken care of.

---

61) **After being assigned to a pediatric care service group you receiving a distressing call. The caller states that she has heard sounds from her neighbor's apartment that made her believe that an infant was being beaten. She discloses that she recently say the infant and that is had blue and black marks all over its body. Your most proper response is:**

A. Instruct the caller to call the police and tell her story to the police.

B. Refer this situation to the proper civil authority that cares for the welfare of children.

C. Relate to the caller that you do not have the authority to act on the basis of a phone call alone.

D. Let the caller know that she cannot do this and that it would be best if she would leave other people's domestic affairs alone.

62) You are assigned as a caseworker in a psychiatric facility. You receive a call from someone who says he has taken pills in an attempt to commit suicide. He is not a patient. You should:

A. Refer the person to a nearby clinic.

B. Collect the person's information and let him know you are here to help. Arrange for emergency help immediately.

C. Get the person in for an appointment. Arrange for a cab to pick him up so you can meet with him.

D. Tell the man to call a suicide hotline for needed assistance.

---

63) A client is worried about going through an upcoming surgery. He has had a similar surgery before and had numerous problems before and after the treatment, including familial conflicts. He is talking about this a lot. The amount of notes you take during this session should be:

A. Record little to no notes at all. You can remember most of his story, which has no pertinent information about his case.

B. Take extensive notes. The details will be beneficial, as the client will understand that you are truly interested in his situation.

C. Take a few notes. You should devote most of your attention to the client and only record definite items.

D. You should record the conversation because there are so many details.

64) One of your clients is a 47-year old diabetic woman who has refused to use her insulin injections. This has resulted in several emergency room visits and three of her diabetic comas. You should:

 A. Get the woman psychiatric treatment due to her rash behavior.
 B. Talk to the man's spouse and demand that they realize the seriousness of the situation.
 C. Arrange for a home health care evaluation so that the man and his spouse can be taught how to inject the insulin.
 D. Tell the client that there are other method of controlling diabetes and recommend dietary changes and holistic medicines.

65) One of your patients is regularly avoiding her medical appointments because she does not think they as important as other problems she is dealing with. Her doctor has assessed that she needs consistent and repeated treatment. You can best convince of the importance of her medical appointments by:

 A. Explaining to her how medical problems are more important than anything else.
 B. Meet with the patient, evaluate how you can help with the other issues and let her know of your capability.
 C. Meet with the patient, but let her know that you can only help her if she consistently makes her medical appointments.
 D. Give her an ultimatum, stating that her case will be dropped if she doesn't get her medical treatments regularly.

66) One of your assignments calls for you to look after a young boy whose parents were hospitalized due to an accident. Which of the following is your primary concern?

    A. Convincing the child to accept adult responsibilities because of his family circumstances

    B. Having fun with the child by engaging in games and developing his imagination to cope with problems

    C. Continually reassuring the child that he has nothing to worry about and that all will be okay

    D. Encouraging the boy to talk about his feelings while reassuring him that you will be there to help him

67) One of your regular patients for the past month has had continual complaints about a serious headache. It is best for you to:

    A. Give the patient pain medication

    B. Suggest that the client receive psychiatric testing

    C. Forward the client to a neurologist

    D. Change the treatment modality

68) You are a working with a client that has similar problems as many of your other patients. Of the below procedures, it would be best to:

    A. Let the client know that they are dealing with problems that many other have.

    B. Try to learn if they are any significant differences that this client has.

    C. Talk about this situation with co-worker.

    D. This is a normal case; handle it just like the rest of your cases.

69) A teenage girl has stopped going to school and prefers to stay home. After verifying that no trauma has occurred and that she is not suffering from school phobia, the caseworker should:

A. Refer the girl to a psychiatrist and insist that she take medication.

B. Arrange tutorial sessions for the girl.

C. Allow the girl to stay at home.

D. Investigate why the girl is resisting school attendance and encourage her parent to assist their daughter to return to school.

70) While sitting in your office, a man abruptly enters in and sits next to your desk. He states that his friend is one of your patients. The patient he refers to has terminal cancer. Your initial response to this man should be:

A. "You are probably worried about your friend, right?"

B. "Thank you for coming in. I'm sorry to tell you, but your friend has terminal cancer."

C. "May I help you?"

D. "You cannot be here without an appointment."

71) During an interview, a client relates his family situation. He says, "Two of my kids are in school but my oldest, who is now 19..." He pauses and does not continue. It would be best for you to:

A. Ask if the oldest child works.

B. Ask if the oldest child left school.

C. Quickly ask about the last child.

D. Patiently wait for the client to continue.

72) A 12-year old boy is ready to be discharged from the hospital after receiving a full-body cast to fix an orthopedic condition. The doctors require that he attend weekly orthopedic sessions at the clinic. The boy's mother is the sole caregiver and you are required to facilitate discharge preparations and follow-up treatments. It would be best if you:

A. Tell the mother to use her vacation time while her son is recovering.
B. Refer the mother to a good rehabilitation center for her son.
C. Suggest that she relinquish her job until her son recovers.
D. Simply assist her in making a decision that will be best for her family.

73) You formerly introduced play therapy to a withdrawn child at a children's day hospital. Nevertheless, the child is currently not responding and seems disinterested. Your best course of action is:

A. Continue the treatment.
B. Review the treatment with your supervisor.
C. Get a medical professional to review the case.
D. Find a caseworker that has a different style of treatment that may help the child.

74) One of your elderly patients is ready to be discharged from hospitalization. He can take care of himself but will need minimal supervision. The best accommodation that you can set up for him is:

A. A rehabilitation facility
B. A nursing home
C. A hospice facility
D. A health-related facility

75) An elderly client ready for discharge will need a great amount of assistance when she returns home. Since she will be living alone, you should recommend:
   A. A companion
   B. A home attendant
   C. A homemaker
   D. A maid

---

76) You have a client who needs certain services that can only be attained from another city agency. The best way to make this referral is to:
   A. Contact the agency via phone and inform them that the client will visit them shortly.
   B. Get the client to contact the agency.
   C. Create a letter for the client and have them take it to the agency.
   D. Execute a release of information with the client. Send this release with a summarization of the client's situation.

---

77) You meet with a client that has just received a diagnosis that her son has childhood diabetes. The client is disturbed and anxious about her child's condition. The best way that you can help this client is by:
   A. Focusing on how the client can help her child.
   B. Completing a psychological assessment of the mother so that you can determine if she can care for the child
   C. Referring her to a betting paying job
   D. Telling the woman to calm down because if she is in a hysterical state, she won't be any help to her child

78) It is generally accepted that a client's value system will not be congruent with the caseworker's. From the following, select the most valid conclusion based on this statement.
   A. Clients are immoral
   B. Caseworkers are usually more cultured than their clients
   C. Caseworkers must never try to get clients to conform to their values
   D. Clients' value systems are inferior, which is why they need caseworkers

79) Many private and public sectors have shown interest in the possibility of combining child welfare and family casework practices. The best reason supporting the merger of the two is:
   A. Families that have experienced childcare issues will not be divided
   B. This will save taxpayers money
   C. New techniques and resources would most likely result from a merger
   D. This will force clients to take care of their children better

80) Usually in social work, the center of attention is placed upon the family. Modern theory dictates that caseworkers:
   A. Get each family member to commit to caseworker help.
   B. Involve the entire family of a client to get better results.
   C. Train families not to interfere with caseworker plans.
   D. Do not involve families in a client's problems.

81) The focal point of an interview is always on the client and their situation. Accordingly, which statement is most correct with respect to interview focus?

A. Caseworkers should get the client to focus on factual information

B. Caseworkers are responsible for assisting clients to focus on anything related to their problems

C. Caseworkers must help clients to focus on their feelings, which often are behind many of the problems they face

D. Caseworkers should not direct the interview; rather, they should allow the client to speak as they wish

82) A complete case record should contain psychological/social facts about the client, the client's attitude towards the agency, their feelings/thoughts about their circumstances, their request, their treatment information and:

A. Full details of their personality and emotional relationships

B. Qualified information for understanding their problem and contributing information to arrive at a viable solution

C. A routine history

D. All of the contact information for friends and relatives that may affect their behavior

83) Select the most accurate statement for providing casework to the medically ill.

    A. The caseworker must have a general understanding of a client's medical problems.

    B. The caseworker's should focus solely on the problem that affects the client's health.

    C. Caseworkers should have a general understanding of the medical treatment for their client's medical problem.

    D. Caseworkers must abstain from involving themselves in the client's medical treatment.

---

84) A married couple that is having difficulties with domestic violence has recently had their child placed in foster care. The caseworker's goals for the couple should be:

    A. To help the family come to decision as to whether they are going to remain married or not

    B. To help the couple understand the role they played in the loss of their child and how they can heal as a couple

    C. To seek treatment for the parents' domestic violence issues while focusing on how to change their family so that it can support and function well enough for the child to return

    D. Educate the parents how this event has scarred their child for life and why they can never behave like this again if they want their child back

85) **A woman has been referred to a community health agency specializing in mental health. Although she has undergone two HIV tests which returned as negative, she is requesting a third. It would be prudent for the caseworker to assess:**

A. The patient's knowledge of HIV

B. Her recent activities that may put her at risk of contracting HIV

C. The reasons why the patient is concerned with testing

D. The patient's mental health stability

86) **An adolescent girl is living with her remarried widowed mother, a 2-year old half-sister, and her stepfather. The adolescent girl is severely neglected and mistreated by both parents. The stepfather doesn't like the girl living with them. If the caseworker has previously been unsuccessful in improving this situation by discussing this matter with the parents, what is the best course of action for the girl's welfare?**

A. Make sure that the girl is placed outside the home and warn the parents that the younger daughter could be taken as well if the situation arises again

B. Prevent further mistreatment of the child by admitting her to foster care. Meanwhile, provide corrective education therapy for the abusive parents

C. Temporary placement of the girl until the stepfather is no longer a part of the family

D. Speak with the stepfather and threaten him if he mistreats the girl again

87) When engaged in a contract with a client, what is the main function of a caseworker?
   A. To be personally responsible for the success of the relationship
   B. To set a clear understanding of the roles and expectations of the caseworker and client
   C. To help the client accept responsibility for the role they will need to play
   D. None of the above

88) Studies reveal that alcoholism has negative effects upon a person's interaction with their family, friends, and society. Caseworkers that are working with a client with a history of alcoholism have the primary responsibility of:
   A. Finding the point of origin of the client's drinking problem, formulating a diagnosis, and creating a viable treatment plan
   B. Helping the client grasp the causes of alcoholism
   C. Assisting the family of the client to be involved in the treatment
   D. Getting the client's closest associates and employer to support their treatment

89) One of your patients reveals that her husband is abusing alcohol and is in danger of losing his job. You should:
   A. Ask to have a meeting with your client's husband
   B. Ascertain if the couple needs casework services
   C. Get in contact with Alcoholics Anonymous
   D. Tell the client to contact her husband's employer to let them know that he is going to get help

90) One of your patients is readmitted to a hospital to receive psychiatric help. He complains that the doctors do not understand him. In this situation, your best course of action is to:

A. Meet with your patient's medical staff and inform them of their mistreatment

B. Reassure the patient that most doctors don't have the time to really understand all of their patients

C. Reassign the patient to a co-worker that is more familiar with psychiatric problems

D. Talk to the client about his concerns and encourage him talk to his doctor about these issues

91) Which of the following is not a main assumption made in casework?

A. There is an interdependency between society and individuals

B. The client must take a responsible role at every step of the casework process

C. Social forces are the main influence on behavior, attitude and opportunity.

D. Restructuring and reorganizing one's personality and environment are required goals

92) When working with any client, a caseworker should:

A. Accept the client in a positive way while remaining objective

B. Understand that most clients will be negative and hard to deal with

C. Be optimistic and permissive

D. Not agree with clients until a long-standing foundation of trust is built

93) Casework is often related to the economic health of the labor market. Which of the listed points represents an accurate statement concerning developments in the labor market?

    A. National defense expansion is a key to long-term job creation

    B. The more overtime that is reported in the overall labor market is a key to increased personal income

    C. The manufacturing industry has increased its employment rate due to incremental utilization of automation

    D. Job applicants have increased due to automation and specialized skill jobs have increased

94) Social Security law states that eligible dependent wives of disabled husbands who are receiving benefits are also entitled to:

    A. 75% of her husband's annual benefits

    B. No more than one third of the husband's annual benefits

    C. A payment equal to her husband's monthly benefits

    D. No more than half of the husband's monthly benefits

95) When meeting a client for the first time who seems reluctant, the best approach for a caseworker is to:

    A. Set firm conditions for the client and get them involved

    B. Take the initiative to tell the client about your personal background and beliefs so that you can put them at ease

    C. Enable the client to express their feelings and ideas, while discerning that time and effort is required to build relationships

    D. Get the client to agree with your ideas so that no problems arise

96) A client has been referred to you by another agency. You have reviewed his case extensively. However, when the client meets with you he begins to relate lengthy details about his situation. Allowing the client to do this is:

A. A waste of time because you already know the details from the report you have from the previous agency

B. Beneficial because the other agency most likely has not included some key details in the report

C. Neither good or bad. It solely depends on how you feel at the time

D. Beneficial because it is important to build a relationship with the client by listening to his concerns and showing personal attention

---

97) Case investigators have the responsibility of gathering and summarizing the observed facts of a family into a formal report. The main purpose of this practice is to:

A. Provide a sound snapshot of the family so that evaluations and plans can be formulated

B. Provide a picture of the family's eligibility for various services

C. Provide a history of the family's situation so that they can understand how a third party's insights can help their family

D. Provide a basis of comparison between families who are and are not at risk

98) A caseworker has opted to make contact with their client's legally responsible relative who is receiving public assistance as well. Which of the following statements is most correct?

    A. The caseworker's actions are beneficial because the relative may be able to help the client with some services

    B. The caseworker's actions are negative because it may create problems between the client and their relative

    C. The caseworker's actions are neither positive or negative

    D. The caseworker's actions are beneficial because the cases can be combined

99) One of your cases involves an unemployed father whose family is receiving public assistance. He explains that he has refused a job offer as a day laborer because he is enrolled in plumber helper training courses. He further relates that when he finishes the training he is confident that he will be able to secure a well-paying job to support his family. Yet, upon further review, you discover that he is on a waiting list for the training and will not be able to initiate the courses until three months later. Should the father's refusal to take the day laborer employment be treated as job refusal?

    A. Yes, since he cannot be sure if he will be able to gain employment after completing the course

    B. No, the man is attempting to gain a viable skill that can increase his earning potential

    C. Yes, the available job will not interfere with the training while he is on the waiting list for the plumbing training

    D. No, he has the right to decline low-paying work if he is trying to attain better skills

100) In instances where applicants are accepted into a public housing project, why should the authorities of those facilities be notified?

    A. Because specialized services are available to tenants of housing projects

    B. To make sure that only the authorized family stated on the application stays in the housing

    C. This allows for reduced rents to be established for the successful applicants

    D. So that the authorities can keep track of how the family is progressing

---

101) As a rule of thumb, it is advisable for caseworkers to be kept abreast of departmental actions, changes in corresponding departments, and general new developments in the industry. Would this practice be beneficial for a welfare department?

    A. No, this additional information would only serve as a distraction

    B. Yes, caseworkers in welfare departments benefit from this practice as it allows them to coordinate with other departments

    C. No, this type of information is not legally transferable between departments

    D. It is neither beneficial or detrimental

---

102) A divorced mother of two whose husband was abusive comes to you. As a caseworker, you must be an active listener. This means that you should primarily:

    A. Offer verbal and nonverbal cues that show continued interest

    B. Make comments that keep the client directly involved in the material

    C. Convey good listening through nonverbal cues

    D. Allow your attention, concern, and empathy to be communicated through your presence and style

103) In a large city, an intake worker determines that an applicant who was referred to this welfare center by the Homeless Women Emergency Assistance Unit of the agency, although apparently in need of assistance, has been referred to the wrong welfare center. The worker should:

A. Refer the applicant back to the Homeless Women Emergency Assistance Unit after the case has been processed and the investigation completed

B. Process the referral and complete the investigation before transferring the case to the appropriate welfare center

C. Process the referral only if the applicant is in need of emergency assistance; otherwise, refer the case to the appropriate center

D. Refer the applicant back to the Homeless Women Emergency Assistance Unit if she is in need of emergency assistance; otherwise, refer her to the appropriate center

---

104) Income resulting from a current court support order may be removed from the budget if the relative under court order ceases to make payments and if they:

A. Present verification to the investigator that they are now financially unable to assist

B. Have not contributed under the court order for twelve consecutive months

C. Have disappeared and it is established that their whereabouts cannot be ascertained

D. Move to another state and refuse to continue their contribution

105) Among the following needy persons, the one NOT eligible to receive veteran assistance is the:

   A. Husband of a veteran, if living with the veteran
   B. Minor grandchild of a veteran, if living with the veteran
   C. Incapacitated child of a deceased veteran
   D. Nonveteran brother or sister of a veteran, if living with the veteran

106) The main difference between public welfare and private social agencies is that in public agencies:

   A. Case records are open to the public
   B. The granting of assistance cannot be sufficiently flexible to meet the varying needs of individual recipients
   C. Only financial assistance may be provided
   D. All policies and procedures must be based upon statutory authorizations

107) An elderly client who is coping with problems in her public housing reveals anxiety-provoking feelings. This client explains that she was abandoned as a child and is fearful that will occur again now. The worker should:

   A. Attempt to sustain the client's functioning to alleviate her anxiety, then proceed to focus on the individual issues at hand once the client is in a calmer state
   B. Involve the client in seeing her anxious state and confront her about this anxiety
   C. Not expect the client to return after this meeting
   D. Expect to reveal a deep psychological stressor that occurred when she was abandoned as a child

108) When an applicant for public assistance is repeatedly told that "everything will be all right," the effect that can usually be expected is that he will:

A. Develop overt negativistic reactions toward the agency

B. Become too closely identified with the interviewer

C. Doubt the interviewer's ability to understand and help with his problems

D. Have greater confidence in the interviewer

109) During an interview, a curious applicant asks several questions about your private life. As the interviewer, you should:

A. Refuse to answer such questions

B. Answer the questions fully

C. Explain that your primary concern is with her problems and that discussion of your personal affairs will not be helpful in meeting her needs

D. Explain that it is the responsibility of the interviewer to ask questions and not to answer them

110) "An interviewer's attention must be directed toward himself as well as toward the person interviewed." This statement means that the interviewer should:

A. Keep in mind the extent to which his own prejudices may influence their judgment

B. Rationalize the statements made by the person being interviewed

C. Gain the respect and confidence of the person interviewed

D. Avoid being too impersonal

111) A good technique for the interviewer to use in an effort to secure reliable data and to reduce the possibility of misunderstanding is to:

A. Secure the desired information by using casual, undirected conversation, enabling the interviewee to talk about himself or herself

B. Use direct questions regularly

C. Extract the desired information from the interviewee by putting him or her on the defensive

D. Explain to the interviewee the information desired and the reason for needing it

112) As a caseworker conducting the first interview with a new public assistance client, you should:

A. Ask questions requiring "yes" or "no" answers in order to simplify the interview

B. Rephrase several of the key questions as a check on his or her previous statements

C. Let him or her tell his or her own story while keeping him or her to the relevant facts

D. Avoid showing any sympathy for the applicant while he or she reveals his or her personal needs and problems

113) Of the sources through which a social service agency can seek information about the family background and economic needs of a particular client, the most important consists of:

A. Records and documents covering the client

B. Interviews with the client's relatives

C. The client's own story

D. Direct contacts with former employers

114) In public assistance agencies, vital statistics are a resource used by caseworkers mainly to:

A. Help establish eligibility through verification of births, deaths, and marriages

B. Help establish eligibility through verification of divorce proceedings

C. Secure proof of unemployment and eligibility for unemployment compensation

D. Secure indices of the cost of living in the larger cities

---

115) Because social caseworkers generally are not trained psychiatrists, they should, when encountering psychiatric problems in the performance of their departmental duties:

A. Ignore such problems because they are beyond the scope of their responsibilities

B. Inform the affected people that they recognize their problems personally but will take no official cognizance of them

C. Ask to be relieved of the cases in which these problems are met and recommend that they be assigned to a psychiatrist

D. Recognize such problems where they exist and make referrals to the proper sources for treatment

---

116) The primary function of any department of social services is to:

A. Refer needy persons to legally responsible relatives for support

B. Enable needy persons to become self-supporting

C. Refer ineligible applicants to private agencies

D. Grant aid to needy eligible clients

117) An individual would be denied assistance for TANF (Temporary Assistance for Needy Families) if they were which of the following?

A. A mother who is married with 3 children from different fathers

B. An individual convicted of a drug felony

C. A teen parent living in an adult supervised setting

D. A person who is on assistance and is cooperative with child support officials

118) The Personal Responsibility and Work Opportunity Reconciliation Act of 1996 ends the federal entitlement of individuals to cash assistance under Title IV-A (AFDC), giving states complete flexibility to determine eligibility and benefits levels. Under the new law, Title IV-A funds are replaced with block grants for Temporary Assistance for Needy Families (TANF). State plans filed with the U.S. Department of Health and Human Services must explain the state's use of these funds. In the plans, a state must:

A. Establish criteria for delivering benefits

B. Deny services as they see fit to reduce budgetary constraints

C. Follow the same regulations all other states; otherwise, there would not be equitable treatment to recipients

D. Explain how it will provide an administrative appeals process for recipients only when questioned in a public court hearing

119) Which of the following lawful permanent residents (LPRs) can lose their green card status?

A. People on health-care programs

B. People receiving food program assistance

C. People who leave the country for more than six months at a time

D. People who avoid long-term care

120) When employment and unemployment figures both decline, the most probable conclusion is that:
   A. The population has reached a condition of equilibrium
   B. Seasonal employment has ended
   C. The labor force has decreased
   D. Payments for unemployment insurance have increased

121) An individual with an IQ of 100 may be said to have demonstrated:
   A. Superior intelligence
   B. Absolute intelligence
   C. Substandard intelligence
   D. Approximately average intelligence

122) The word deviant means:
   A. Ordinary
   B. Crafty
   C. Insubordinate
   D. Unacceptable

123) The technical term used to express the ratio between mental and chronological age is called the:
   A. Mentality rating
   B. Intelligence quotient
   C. Psychometric standard
   D. Achievement index

124) Dementia was once referred to as:

A. Mental retardation

B. Senility

C. Stupidity

D. Gerontology

QUESTIONS 125-127 ARE BASED ON THE FOLLOWING PASSAGE.

Aid to dependent children shall be given to a parent or other relative as herein specified for the benefit of a child or children under 16 years of age or of a minor or minors between 16 and 18 years of age if in the judgment of the administrative agency: **(1)** the granting of an allowance will be in the interest of such child or minor; **(2)** the parent or other relative is a fit person to bring up such child or minor so that his physical, mental, and moral well-being will be safeguarded; **(3)** aid is necessary to enable such parent or other relative to do so; **(4)** such child or minor is a resident of the state on the date of application for aid; and **(5)** such minor between 16 and 18 years of age is regularly attending school in accordance with the regulations of the department. An allowance may be granted for the aid of such child or minor who has been deprived of parental support or care by reason of death, continued absence from the home, or physical or mental incapacity of parent, and who is living with his father, mother, grandfather, grandmother, brother, sister, stepfather, stepmother, stepbrother, stepsister, uncle, or aunt. In making such allowances, consideration shall be given to the ability of the relative making application and of any other relatives to support and care for or to contribute to the support and care of such child or minor. In making all such allowances, it shall be made certain that the religious faith of the child or minor shall be preserved and protected.

125) On the basis of the passage, which of the following statements is the most accurate?

  A. Mary Doe, mother of John, age 18, is entitled to aid for her son if he is attending school regularly

  B. Evelyn Stowe, mother of Eleanor, age 13, is not entitled to aid for Eleanor if she uses her home for immoral purposes

  C. Ann Roe, cousin of Helen, age 14, is entitled to aid for Helen if the latter is living with her

  D. Peter Moe, uncle of Henry, age 15, is not entitled to aid for Henry if the latter is living with him

---

126) The passage is concerned primarily with:

  A. The financial ability of people applying for public assistance

  B. Compliance on the part of applicants with the "settlement" provisions of the law

  C. The fitness of parents or other relatives to bring up physically, mentally, or morally delinquent children between the ages of 16 and 18

  D. Eligibility for aid to families with dependent children

---

127) The passage is probably an excerpt from

  A. A city's administrative code

  B. A state's social welfare law

  C. The Federal Security Act

  D. A city's charter

128) The length of residence required to make a person eligible for the various forms of public assistance available in the United States:

   A. Is the same in all states but different when among various public assistance programs in a given state

   B. Is the same in all states and among different public assistance programs in a given state

   C. Is the same in all states for different categories.

   D. Varies among states and among different assistance programs in a given state

129) A person who knowingly brings a needy person from one state into another state for the purpose of making him or her a public charge is generally guilty of:

   A. Violation of the Displaced Persons Act

   B. Violation of the Mann Act

   C. A felony

   D. A misdemeanor

130) Adoption is the process through which:

   A. The natural parents' rights and obligations toward their child are always maintained

   B. The adoptive parents assume all rights and obligations once a child has been adopted

   C. The natural or birth parents are always legally responsible for their child

   D. The natural or birth parents maintain all the obligations, and rights between a parent and child

131) Any person or organization soliciting donations in public places in New York City is required to have a license issued by the:
   A. Police department
   B. Department of Sanitation
   C. Division of Labor Relations
   D. Department of Social Services

132) In the population at large individuals who tend to be at the greatest risk for contracting HIV are:
   A. single women from homes with household incomes over $90,000
   B. African-American males over 30
   C. Asian-American males
   D. young disadvantaged women, particularly African-American women

133) Proper utilization of the term *carious* would involve reference to what?
   A. Teeth
   B. Curiosity
   C. Shipment of food packages to needy persons in Europe.
   D. Hazardous situations

134) The medical term for "hardening of the arteries" is:
   A. Carcinoma
   B. Arthritis
   C. Thrombosis
   D. Arteriosclerosis

135) If the characteristics of a person were being studied by competent observers, it would be expected that their observations would differ most markedly with respect to their evaluation of the person's:

A. Intelligence
B. Height
C. Temperamental characteristics
D. Weight

136) Although malnutrition is generally associated with poverty, dietary studies of population groups in the United States reveal that:

A. Malnutrition is most often due to a deficiency of nutrients
B. There has been overemphasis of the causal relationship between poverty and malnutrition
C. Malnutrition is found among people with sufficient money to be well fed.
D. A majority of the population in all income groups is undernourished.

137) One of the most common characteristics of the chronic alcoholic is:

A. Low intelligence level.
B. Wanderlust.
C. Psychosis.
D. Egocentricity.

138) You are working with Ms. Smothers, a stroke victim who has two children and has suffered the death of her 3-month-old baby after ignoring her doctor's orders not to get pregnant again. The clinic *OB/GYN* staff has told her that they consider her attempting to have another child to be a risk. Ms. Smothers insists on trying to have another child because this loss has been devastating for her 10-year-old daughter and 8-year-old son. You meet with the children and they show no signs of depression and seem well-adjusted. You would recommend:

A. That this patient consider not having any more children as she is inflicting great pressure on her children and projecting her feelings of loss onto them

B. That this patient consider not having any more children as she has an increased risk of giving birth to a child with severe birth effects as a result of her health condition

C. That the patient be followed for ongoing counseling to help her deal with her loss and understand her reasons for wanting to go against her doctor's orders in order to endure another high-risk pregnancy

D. That this patient consider not having any more children as she is inflicting great pressure on her body and that she is at a great risk for having another, possibly more severe, strokr

139) Because circumstances under which applications are made to a Department of Welfare are so often the result of financial conditions, the nature of home relief assistance is usually:

A. Monetory
B. Monetary
C. Monitory
D. Monitary

140) An unfortunate occurrence that threatens to happen immediately is one that is:

  A. Immanent
  B. Immenent
  C. Imminent
  D. Omenent

---

141) Strabismus is usually associated with:

  A. Hearing
  B. Sight.
  C. Blood pressure
  D. Bone structure

---

142) Which of the following is the best example of recidivism?

  A. John Smith is released on parole and begins to sell drugs, after which he is arrested and placed back into prison
  B. John Smith is released on parole and declines an opportunity to sell drugs from an old contact
  C. John Smith is released on parole and begins to sell drugs. He avoids getting arrested and becomes a high-profile drug dealer
  D. John Smith is released on parole and tries to get arrested and placed back into prison

143) A personality restraint imposed upon one psychological activity by another, which is harmful and may lead to mental illness, is known as:

  A. Expression
  B. Transference
  C. Symbiosis
  D. Inhibition

144) When a public assistance agency assigns its most experienced interviewers to conduct initial interviews with applicants, the most important reason for its action is that:

A. Experienced workers are always older, and therefore command the respect of applicants

B. The applicant may be given a complete understanding of the procedures to be followed and the time involved in obtaining assistance payments

C. Applicants with fraudulent intentions will be detected and prevented from obtaining further services from the agency

D. The applicant may be given an understanding of the purpose of the assistance program and of the bases for granting assistance in addition to the routine information

145) The most significant and pervasive indicator of alcoholism is:

A. Early morning drinking
B. Blackouts
C. Defensive behavior
D. Withdrawal

146) The least likely symptom of depression is:

A. Disturbances in orientation and thinking
B. Sadness and hopelessness
C. Insomnia
D. Disturbances in food intake and elimination

147) An emotionally mature adult is a person who has:

A. No need to be dependent on others and who is proud of his or her independence and ability to help others who are dependent on him or her

B. Little need for satisfaction from social relationships and who is able to live comfortably alone

C. Insight into and understanding of his or her emotional needs and strengths

D. Considerable need to depend on others and to be loved and cared for

148) In making a social study of an application for service, a thorough review of the previous history of a family's contacts with the Department of Social Service contained in the department's case records is:

A. Not important because current eligibility is based on contemporary facts and these will have to be secured and verified anew

B. Important because the caseworker can anticipate whether he or she will have trouble with the family in determining their eligibility by learning how they behaved in the past

C. Important but should not be made until after the caseworker has formed his or her own opinion in personal contact because previous workers' opinions may prejudice him or her

D. Important so that current investigation can be focused on such additional information as is needed, with a minimum of time and effort and in a manner that will be of help to the family

149) **"The fact that an individual receives his means of support from an assistance agency rather than from wages or other recognized income is a fact of difference from his neighbors that cannot be denied or dismissed lightly. There is a deeply rooted tradition in this country that the person who is 'anybody' supports himself by his own efforts, that there is something wrong about getting one's support from a source created by the whole. Thus, the individual who gets his support from a social agency is considered in a group apart and different from his neighbors." Relating this statement to practice, you should:**

A. Recognize the client as different and give such casework service as will enable him or her to become a member of the self-supporting community as soon as possible

B. Explain to each client that you understand the difficulties of asking for and receiving help, and there is no need to be self-conscious with you

C. Analyze your own feelings toward the particular client to secure some insight into how you personally relate to this cultural pattern and to the client, and what your own attitudes towards dependency are

D. Make strenuous efforts to change the cultural pattern of the community, which is harmful to so large a part of it

150) Mr. Wilson comes to a Department of Social Services to request assistance. He matter-of-factly presents his situation; methodically submits bills, receipts, and other verification documents; and then asks how much help he will get and how soon he may expect it. This behavior should indicate to an alert caseworker that Mr. Wilson:

A. Is probably a relatively secure adult with considerable strength and capacity for independence

B. Is probably a chronically dependent person who has been through this routine so often before that he has the procedure memorized

C. Is a naturally aggressive individual accustomed to sweeping everything before him in the accomplishment of his purpose

D. Has probably prepared a fictitious story in order to hide his real situation and "beat" the eligibility requirements

Answer Key & Rationales

1) D: They can provide the child with a food basket where he can keep his healthy snacks and they can refill the basket when it is nearing empty.

Supporting the child and helping him learn that he will not go without food is important in helping him overcome the neglect he experienced.

2) A: Discuss with each client the potential risks, benefits, and consequences of receiving services via electronic media.

It is important to discuss the risks and potential consequences with clients so that clients are aware how services delivered via electronic media differ from face-to-face contact.

3) B: Talk to the client about the possible dangers of alcohol withdrawal and allow the client to make his own decision about whether or not to seek medical help.

Unless there is a medical emergency, the proper course is to explain the possible risks to the client and discuss whether or not he wants to seek medical treatment.

4) D: His improvement during his hospitalization may actually give him the energy to complete suicide.

His improvement in the hospital puts him at a higher risk because he may now have the energy to plan and follow through with suicide.

5) B: Talk to the client about whether or not she would want any information disclosed and the possible implications of disclosing information.

It is appropriate to discuss with the client whether or not she wants her teacher to be made aware of the assault, and she should be warned of the possible implications.

6) C: "You are free to choose whether or not you want to try to regain custody of the children."

It is appropriate to tell the client that he has the right to choose how to respond to child protective services.

7) A: "Do you prefer sex with men, women, or both?"

This question, asked in a non-judgmental fashion, is the most effective way to encourage a discussion of sexual preference.

8) A: The client may be superficially compliant with treatment to try gain approval but may struggle to make lasting change.

Clients with dependent personality disorder typically need approval and reassurance, so they often try to appear cooperative to please the social worker.

9) D: Precontemplation

All these strategies are most likely to be effective with a client who is precontemplative.

10) A: Assist them in establishing treatment goals to help them learn to improve their communication and resolve conflict.

It is correct to help them learn new skills that they can use to address the problem of disagreements over chores as well as other problems in their relationship.

112

11) C: Behavior therapy

Behavior therapy is the best fit because it allows the caseworker and the client to address the behavior associated with the depression. The client will therefore be able to identify and possibly avoid behaviors that promote depression.

12) C: Schizophrenia

13) C: Confidentiality

Client confidentiality would be the appropriate violation. Caseworkers must be careful not to encroach upon this fundamental right.

14) B: Competency

Agencies may mandate that their employees keep abreast of training and updates in the industry. This takes place to improve the competency of the caseworker.

15) C: Visual

Communication with clients dealing with autism can be difficult. In this example, the caseworker is communicating visually with the child.

16) A: Anti-social personality disorder

17) D: Religious discrimination

Workers are covered by laws that protect them against religious intolerance. In this case, the worker's religious rights were hindered by the employer.

18) A: When it interferes with problem solving.

Anxiety disorder is apparent when an individual feels that the problems or issues will continue without letup. Continued thoughts and emotional response to these problems cause the person to forgo problem solving.

19) D: Initiate public hearings

20) A: Social equality

21) A: An unconscious attempt to protect oneself from an identity-threatening feeling

22) C: Imaginary

23) A: Narcissistic personality disorder

24) C: Both A and B

25) B:Source

The Source Credibility theory states that people more likely to be persuaded when a source presents itself as credible. For example, Bochner and Insko found that people were more likely to trust a sleep expert than a non-sleep expert on matters surrounding sleep.

26) D: Stereotyping

The theory of stereotyping involves taking the general characteristic of a group as a means to categorize a larger community.

27) B:The social worker should protect the client's anonymity.

Even when discussing research with other colleagues care must be taken to ensure that all participants' confidentiality is upheld.

28) A: Macro

29) C: To ensure his staff provides professional services to the greatest extent possible.

In times of emergency, social workers should assist clients and city municipal authorities to improve general safety.

30) A: Impulse control

31) C: Empathy

32) B: Cognitive therapy

33) A: Analyze the behaviors

34) D: All of the above

35) D: Yes.

The social worker can terminate services if there is no imminent danger to the client.

36) B:Behaviorism theory

37) D: Avoidant personality disorder

38) D: Oppositional defiant disorder

39) D: All of the above

40) A: Self-perception

41) B: It is the most general answer and describes the broad outlines of the policy's intention in regard to children at risk.

42) B: This is a factual question and is unambiguous.

43) B: A supervisor is legally responsible for cases under supervision and shares personal responsibility with the supervisee.

The agency is also liable since their agents performed the actions leading to the alleged damage.

44) C: This is a fact question.

NOS is an abbreviation for Not Otherwise Specified.

45) B: The youth's functioning seems appropriate for his IQ and his achievement are within normal range.

The question refers to the development of a plan and the answer should reflect a planning response. Given the youth's age and high functioning, it is likely that he can eventually find employment and live independently. This should be a focus of the social worker.

46) A: Caseworkers must keep good appointment schedules.

Appointments should stay intact and only be interrupted in cases where an emergency has arisen. When clients have additional issues to discuss, a new appointment should be schedule to address that concern.

47) D: The adoptive parents must be fully aware of the baby's background so that they can properly care for the child.

Therefore, caseworkers must be direct and fully disclose vital details about adoptions.

48) A: While intoxicated a client can be non-attentive, defiant or dangerous.

The best approach is to reschedule the meeting with the client when he is sober.

49) D: While it is your responsibility to discuss the client's viewpoint, it is equally important that the client grasp society's viewpoint as well.

Caseworkers should not disclose their personal ideas. Help the client to understand the consequences of willfully not accepting employment and explain societal work values.

50) A: Due to confidentiality it is proper to get the client's consent to speak with their probation officer before contacting the law officer.

A caseworker will not be able to assist the client with decisions without communicating with their probation officer.

51) C: The primary concern for the caseworker is to understand why the client is taking their position.

After assessing this, one can discern how to best help her.

52) A: Casework protocol prevents the lending of money to clients by a facility or its individual employees.

Caseworkers must delicately explain that this is not permissible to the client so that a good relationship is maintained.

53) C: Asking investigative questions is an integral process of casework.

Its main purpose is to gather information which is to be accepted as true to determine eligibility for public assistance.

54) B: Finding out the client's rationale behind their decision is a caseworker's primary concern.

In this way, you may be able to help the client with specific resources.

55) B: Rephrasing is a good technique to improve communication between you and the client.

It allows the client to rethink the question and describe their answer differently.

56) C: When suicide is an issue, it is the responsibility of a caseworker to follow up.

In the case of a minor, the parent must be informed of the situation.

57) C: It is always best for the client to make the decision about their residence themselves.

If guidance is needed, the caseworker can help the client arrive at a decision.

58) B: Children find it difficult to hide their feelings, yet they may not be able to communicate them well.

Therefore, good caseworker observation can help to assess certain truths that are not communicated.

59) C: In the given situation, the best casework technique is to allow the client to describe the abuse when they are ready.

Focusing on the practical help that can be rendered is most advantageous.

60) C: Taking a supportive and understanding role in this situation is conducive to achieving the best outcome for the patient and his grandchildren.

Assisting him to make her best judgment call for his grandchildren's care is ideal.

61) B: Caseworker protocol dictates that all problems that are not the responsibility of the department must be referred to the agency that handles the issue.

In this case, a child welfare agency should be contacted.

62) B: All suicide threats must be taken seriously.

This situation calls for the caseworker to keep the person calm while getting immediate help.

63) C: Note taking depends upon each situation.

In this case, it is best to record only a few notes while giving attention to the client. The nature of the discussion is primarily a person one so extensive notes will only serve as a distraction and likely will not furnish referencing material.

64) C: Many patients are unsure of how to administer self-medicating treatments and will avoid them.

Educating the couple is the best way to prevent future medical emergencies because it empowers them to take control of the situation.

65) B: Helping the client deal with the nonmedical problem will allow her to focus on the medical ones.

First you must understand the non-medical issues, discern their importance, and help the client cope or solve these problems. Then you can help them to realize the seriousness of the medical appointments.

66) D: In these circumstances, the caseworker will need to assist the child with coping and understanding the situation.

The caseworker must also reassure the child that he will be cared for and that adults are ready available to help in any way possible.

67) C: Casework should never be confused with medical treatment. Refer clients that need medical attention, no matter how minor, to trained professionals.

68) B: Although problems may be similar, every situation is unique and may require a different solution.

Caseworkers must learn as much as possible about each client before working on a solution.

69) D: Any changes in the behavior of a child can indicate severe problems.

In this situation, it is important for the caseworker to check with the parents and encourage them to work with the school.

70) C: Although the man apparently is privy to his friend's medical situation, you still are unaware of the reason for his visit.

It is appropriate to ask him how you can help him.

71) D: Sometime clients will get lost in describing a topic due to another thought.

Allow clients to work through their thought process by avoiding leading or prompting their speech if they pause.

72) A primary concept in social work is to assist clients to understand consequences, make decisions, and take responsibility for their decisions.

This case calls for the caseworker to help the mother arrive at the best decision herself.

73) B: When dealing with a therapy type that is new, like play therapy, it is important to grasp how your techniques and awareness can improve.

Meeting with a supervisor can be insightful to your ability to recognize child behavior indicators.

74) D: An elder individual who is capable of managing their needs with minimal supervision is best suited for a health-related facility.

75) B: In this case, a home attendant is necessary.

Please review the glossary for a detailed definition.

76) D: It is always necessary to obtain a release of confidential information before forwarding it to a government agency.

The best way to expedite the process is to acquire the release, gather all the information that will be required by the other agency, and set up an appointment for the client.

77) A: Having the client focus on helping her child is the main objective.

This is best accomplished by assisting her with solving the problem while alleviating her fears concerning the diagnosis.

78) C: A basic concept of casework involves not imposing one's personal moral conviction upon any client.

79) C: Of the listed choices, the best answer is the resulting resources that could arise from the combination of the entities.

80) B: Modern theories in casework state that the family unit is a great help in client problem resolution.

Studies show that the support system created by the family is highly beneficial to assisting clients to accept and improve their situation.

81) B: Helping the client focus on the actual situation is the best practice technique because it is the most conducive to resolution.

82) B: In order for a case record to be useful, it must contain information that is necessary for understanding the problem and any variables that are vital to gaining a solution.

83) A: A general understanding of the client's medical issues will help the caseworker to be able to discuss accurately the client's problems.

Without this knowledge, it would be impossible for the caseworker to help the client come to a resolution.

84) C: Changes that are needed are most easily addressed when the family works together while undergoing treatment.

This way, their awareness of domestic violence increases and they have a greater opportunity to approach their difficulties as a untied family.

85) C: In this situation, gaining insight into the woman's concerns will help the caseworker to provide education concerning HIV and its associated risks.

86) B: For this case, a discussion with the parents has not been helpful.

Therefore, placement of the girl in foster care is necessary until the parents are able to provide proper care.

87) B: The client/caseworker relationship should be one in which both parties understands what is expected.

There should be clear comprehension of how they are to work together.

88) A: The primary responsibility of the caseworker in this situation is to provide a full range of assistance.

89) B: Getting both husband and wife the help they need individually will help them to be able understand what they are capable of and act.

90) D: The client's physician is able to gain insight into the client/caseworker relationship if the caseworker encourages the patient to speak with his doctor.

91) C: Case work theory and practice concentrates on solving individual and family behavior problems and attitudes, on obtaining individual and family participation in the solution of problems affecting their lives, and on helping to change their environments for the welfare of client(s).

It is not generally concerned with attempts to reconstruct total personalities or total environments.

92) A: When working with a client, a caseworker must always provide an environment free from judgment, but be aware that there is more to this client than what he or she presents.

It helps to be reserved when developing an understanding of a client and his or her patterns.

93) D: The demands of the labor market have resulted in the increase in the number of unskilled or semiskilled persons looking for jobs because automation and computerization have made their former jobs obsolete.

At the same time, the need has grown for persons with specialized skills required by the newly computer-automated industries. The influx of women into the job market has further increased the number of job applicants.

94) D: The wife of a husband declared disabled and receiving benefits under the Social Security law can receive no more than one half of her husband's payments.

This can also work the other way: if the wife is disabled and covered by disability payments, the husband can also collect up to one half of the amount involved.

95) C: Enable the client to express their feelings and ideas, while discerning that time and effort is required to build relationships.

96) D: Beneficial, because it is important to build a relationship with the client by listening to his concerns and showing personal attention.

97) A: Provide a sound snapshot of the family so that evaluations and plans can be formulated.

98) A: The caseworker's actions are beneficial because the relative may be able to help the client with some services.

99) C: Yes, the available job will not interfere with the training while he is on the waiting list for the plumbing training.

100) A: Because specialized services are available to tenants of housing projects.

101) B: Yes, caseworkers in welfare departments benefit from this practice as it allows them to coordinate with other departments.

102) D: This client needs the attention, concern, and empathy that you can provide.

By providing this, you will establish a relationship communicated through your presence and style.

103) B: Here is a circumstance in which an apparent error has been made by a worker from social services.

Therefore, it should be corrected without further inconveniencing the client and in a manner that will not reduce the confidence of the client in the operation of the agency as a whole. If a client mistakenly walks into the wrong unit of the agency, she should be directed to the proper unit even if it is some distance away. However, if the client has been sent to the wrong location by a social services worker, proper corrective measures should be instituted at once.

104) C: The client's budget provides that under a court order the client receive a degree of financial support from the relative.

Agency policy generally provides that the amount remain in the budget unless the court removes or modifies its order or the agency is certain the order will not be followed and the client will not be receiving that amount of money. Choices (A) and (B) do not provide that assurance. When the relative moves to another state, as in choice (D), there are reciprocal agreements between states to provide that the court-ordered amount of money will still be made available for the client. Only when a relative has disappeared and an exhaustive search for his or her whereabouts has proved unsuccessful can the income from the relative be removed from the budget.

105) D: Most cities and of the passage shows that social workers states, if providing for veteran assistance, do not consider nonveteran brothers or sisters living with the veteran who is eligible for such assistance as eligible for that form of assistance.

106) D: The chief difference between public welfare and private social work agencies is that all major policies and procedures pursued by public agencies have their basis in statutes passed by the legislature of the governmental jurisdiction concerned and are signed by the head of that jurisdiction.

107) A: By attempting to sustain the client's functioning to alleviate her anxiety, you can then focus on the individual issues at hand once the client is in a calmer state.

This allows the client to feel safe and heard.

108) C: Applicants for public assistance, like most people, have problems that are real and complex.

By telling a client "everything will be all right," you are misleading the client and making him doubt your ability to understand the complexity of the problem and the difficulty in solving it. This may result in the client's loss of confidence in your interest and competence.

109) C: The best way to handle the situation presented is merely to remind the client that together you are focusing solely on her problems.

A discussion of your personal affairs will not be useful in resolving any of these problems.

110) A: The quotation reminds the interviewer that one's personal attitude and beliefs, unless understood and accounted for, may hinder efforts to find a solution to the client's problems.

111) D: The best way to obtain reliable information and lessen the chance of misunderstandings in case work interviewing is to make sure that the client understands both the reasons for the question and how the truthful, accurate answer will help solve problems or establish eligibility for public assistance.

Choice (A) may result in misunderstandings, choice (B) in prevarication, and choice (C) in resentment.

112) D: Basic case work interviewing in a public setting requires that the worker generally assume that information the client furnishes is truthful unless reliable information or documentation to the contrary is in the worker's possession at the time the interview is being conducted, or unless the client's information is so contrary to common sense that its truthfulness must be explored.

This does not mean that certain required basic data to establish eligibility must be left unverified.

113) C: The primary source for information about the family background and economic needs of a client is simply the client.

Relatives, friends, records, employers, etc., are secondary sources and may be consulted to verify certain information given by the client, but it is only from the client that the complete picture can be obtained.

114) A: Vital statistics are kept by a local or state government agency and provide official records of births, deaths, and marriages in that locality.

Such official information is essential in giving proof of information, such as a client's age or parentage of a child, which is often needed in establishing eligibility for certain types of public assistance.

115) D: A good caseworker must know when the help of a professional in another discipline is needed and refer the client to this other source.

At the same time, the worker must remain responsible for the entire case and coordinate activities with the other professional.

116) D: The chief duty of a public welfare agency is to investigate the eligibility of a person or family applying for public assistance and to grant such assistance to those found eligible.

117) B: The federal law limits the provision of TANF and requires that a family's benefit be reduced if parents do not cooperate with child support officials, denies assistance to individuals convicted of a drug felony, denies assistance for ten years to any person convicted of fraud in the receipt of benefits in two or more states, and denies assistance to teen parents not living in an adult-supervised setting.

118) A: The Personal Responsibility and Work Opportunity Reconciliation Act of 1996 ends the federal entitlement of individuals to cash assistance under Title IV-A (AFDC), giving state complete flexibility to determine eligibility and benefits levels.

Under this law, Title IV-A funds are replaced with block grants for Temporary Assistance for Needy Families (TANF). State plans filed with the U.S. Department of Health and Human Services must explain the states' use of these funds.

119) C: LPRs who leave the country for more than six months at a time can be questioned about whether they are "public charges" when they return, and the use of cash welfare or long-term care may be considered.

In very rare circumstances, LPRs who use cash welfare' or long-term care within their first five years in the United States for reasons (such as an illness or disability) that existed before their entry to the United States could be considered deportable as a public charge.

120) C: When there are both fewer employees and fewer unemployed, the labor force-i.e., the number of persons available for work-has decreased.

121) D: An IQ of 100 is may demonstrative of average intelligence.

IQs below the 100 mark are demonstrative of varying degrees of substandard intelligence. IQs above 100 are demonstrative of varying degrees of superior intelligence.

122) D: Deviant behavior is one of the features of certain types of mental illness.

123) B: An intelligence quotient is derived by dividing the mental age of the individual being tested by his/her chronological age.

124) B: Dementia was once called senility. It is now defined as a gradual worsening in memory and other mental abilities as a result of brain damage, rather than as the natural result of aging. A common form of dementia is Alzheimer's disease.

125) B: The passage clearly states that eligibility for AFDC is conditioned upon whether the parent of other relatives applying for the assistant is a "fit" person to bring up such a child so that his "physical, mental, or moral well-being will be safeguarded."

Such a situation is not indicated in the situation described in the correct answer. Note that choice (A) is incorrect because the child is 18years of age. Choices (C) and (D) are not true according to the passage.

126) D: The passage discusses the facts that must be considered and the rules that apply in establishing eligibility in the category of public assistance called Aid to Families with Dependent Children.

127) B: The passage concerns the legal requirements for eligibility for the Aid to Families with Dependent Children's category of public assistance.

This program is a statewide program, and the statutes governing such a program would be found in the state's welfare laws.

128) D: Public assistance is determined by individual states based on that state's particular residency requirements.

129) D: In most states, the action indicated in the sentence would make the person who committed such action guilty of a misdemeanor.

None of the other answer choices are appropriate for the action described.

130) B: Adoption is the process through which the natural parents' rights and obligations toward their child is terminated, and the adoptive parents assume these rights and obligations.

Once a child has been adopted, the natural or birth parents are no longer responsible for their child; the obligations that they have toward their child, likewise, cease to exist. The adoptive parents responsible for the child and all the obligations and rights between a parent and child are established between them.

131) D: The social service agency in most localities is responsible for validating charities within its areas.

132) D: Young disadvantaged women, particularly African American women, are being infected with HIV at younger ages and at higher rates than their male counterparts.

133) A: Carious is defined as "affected with caries," which is another term for tooth decay.

134) D: Arteriosclerosis is defined as "a chronic disease characterized by abnormal thickening or hardening of the arteries."

135) C: Height and weight are easily and accurately measured.

Standardized tests result in marks that measure intelligence with sufficient accuracy so that most experts utilizing such tests will come out with the same evaluation of a person's intelligence. Observances of temperamental characteristics are not scientifically measured, and experts frequently differ in their evaluations depending on the tests used, the expert's own biases, and the situation surrounding the observations.

136) C: Dietary studies, especially in the United States, show that many people, although affluent enough to feed themselves properly, suffer from malnutrition because they prefer to eat foods lacking in nutritional value (i.e., "junk food") rather than nutritive foods and/or diet-conscious but not diet-wise foods.

137) D: Studies of chronic alcoholics show many such individuals to be concerned with and unwilling or unable to focus on problems outside of their own immediate concern.

138) C: This patient needs to be followed for ongoing counseling to help her deal with her loss and understand her reasons for wanting to go against her doctor's orders in order to endure another high-risk pregnancy.

As a result, she is causing her family, her future family, and herself great undue stress.

139) B: The correct spelling is monetary, which means "of or relating to money or to the mechanisms by which it is supplied to and circulates in the economy."

140) C: The correct spelling is imminent, which means "about to take place or hanging threateningly above one's head."

141) B: Strabismus is a disorder of vision due to the inability of one or both eyes to turn from the normal position.

Therefore, both eyes cannot be directed at the same point or object at the same time (i.e., squint or cross-eye).

142) A: Recidivism is when an individual has a chronic relapse or a tendency to relapse into a criminal or antisocial behavior.

143) D: Inhibition is the correct word for the mental process that restrains an action.

Look up the meanings of the words given in the other answer choices to be sure you understand their psychological and scientific meanings.

144) D: At the initial interview with an applicant for public assistance, the purpose of the programs, the basic rules for eligibility, and the responsibilities in proving eligibility must be explained and understood.

The ability to impart this data to a new applicant and to set the proper tone for future relations between the applicant and the agency requires skills that are best taught by experience.

145) B: The most significant and pervasive indicator of alcoholism is blackouts.

Blackouts are periods where individuals lose conscious memory of their actions and behavior while in a highly intoxicated state.

146) A: The least likely symptom of depression is disturbances in orientation and thinking.

147) C: One who is emotionally mature knows himself or herself, including any emotional weaknesses and strengths and, to an extent, his or her reasons.

The other answer choices may be true of some emotionally mature people, but these characteristics do not differentiate them from emotionally immature individuals.

148) D: A caseworker should thoroughly examine case records concerning a family's past contacts with the agency under the circumstances described because it will avoid duplication of investigation verification.

Furthermore, discussion that has been thoroughly investigated and verified can then lead to concentration on current problems and/or changes in the situation, e.g., the death of the father of a family need not be discussed if previously verified.

149) C: The quotation concerns the fact that society in general feels that people on public assistance are somehow set apart and are different from the rest of society.

It is most important that a caseworker in a public agency examines personal attitudes and prejudices toward public assistance in general and his or her own caseload in particular in order to be able to relate objectively to clients as individuals who are able to be understood and assisted.

150) A: In this situation, Mr. Wilson displays ideal client behavior, and it can be deduced that he is a relatively secure individual with the strength of character needed to remain independent and possibly to become self-supporting again.

Glossary of Common Test Terms

Below are useful terms and definitions that you may find useful to your test preparation. Many students find it helpful to create flashcards of the glossary for improved memorization.

Active case – A case where recipient(s) are receiving public assistance

ADA – Americans with Disabilities Act (ADA). Established in 1990, it prohibits discriminatory activities against individuals with a disability. The law covers any mental or physical impairment that significantly limits one's ability to engage in normal life activity.

Adoption – A legal proceeding in which an adult person takes another adult or minor into the relationship of child and thereby obtains the rights and incurs the responsibilities of parent with respect to the adopted person. Laws that protect the child, natural parents, and adoptive parents control the adoption process. Two types of adoption are recognized in the law: voluntary and adoption through a legitimate agency.

Advocacy - The act of mediating on behalf of an individual or a group to defend or support access to resources and services

Ambivalence – A set of simultaneous and contradictory emotions about a person, an issue, or person

Anti-social disorder – behavior where an individual shows disregard for his safety and demonstrates violent behaviors

Applicant – A person who applies for public assistance and care, either directly or through a representative

Applicant form – A form required by local and/or state and federal agencies responsible for providing public assistance. Applicants for such assistance fill out the form. It is the applicant's statement of relevant facts and is used in helping determine his or her potential eligibility for financial assistance.

Application rejected – A statistical definition used by many public assistance agencies denoting that an application for public assistance was rejected at the time of the initial interview without further investigation

Assignment – A transfer to another of any property, real or personal, in possession or in action; or of any estate or right therein

Authorization form (regular) – Used to authorize assistance for two or more issues of a recurring allowance, to a maximum of six monthly issues, for all types of assistance

Authorized agency – Any agency, corporation, institution, or other organization incorporated or organized under the laws of the state. With corporate power or empowered by law to care for, to place out, or to board out children; and that actually has its place of business in this state. They must be approved, visited, inspected, and supervised by the State Board of Social Welfare or submit and consent to the approval , visitation, inspection and supervision of the Board as to any and all acts in relation to the welfare of children.

Basic case name and number – The name and case number of the eligible payee designated as the responsible head in either a single case or a composite case

Basic case record – The case folder maintained either for a case consisting of one eligible payee (single case) or for a case consisting of two or more eligible payees (composite case) where members of the household are budgeted together as a family unit

Board out – To arrange for the care of a child with a nonrelative family within the second degree of the parents of such child where payments are made or are agreed to be made for the child's care

Boarder – A person who receives and pays for meals in a client's home but does not reside with the client or pay rent

Boarder-lodger – A person who lives in the home of a client, receives meals there, and pays for room and board

Budget deficit – The difference between items in the budget that are required by individuals or families and the income or other resources in cash or in kind available to such individuals or families to meet their needs. The amount of the regular recurring grant is the budget deficit

Case closed – A statistical definition denoting that public assistance has been terminated

Case number – The serial number assigned to a public assistance case. The case number includes a prefix, the abbreviation of the type of assistance, the suffix, and the abbreviation of the form of charge e.g. AB 100001 LC; OAA214032 PSC

Case record – A folder containing the application form, verification sheet, face sheet (when applicable), recorded material, and other relevant information including required forms and correspondence. This is sometimes referred to as the case folder.

Caseload – The total number of cases assigned to one worker

Child Welfare – A field of practice in case work where the concern is the protection and strengthening of families

CHIP – The United States Department of Health and Human Services administers the Children's Health Insurance Program (CHIP). Its purpose is to cover uninsured children whose families earn too much to qualify for Medicaid but not enough to pay for health insurance. Federal and state governments finances CHIP. Each state government determines eligibility requirements based on general guidelines provided by the federal government.

Client (recipient) – A person in receipt of public assistance and care

Collateral visits – Visits to friends, relatives, landlords, former employers, etc. to verify information given by the applicant or client to establish initial or continued eligibility for public assistance.

Composite case – The case of a family group in which there is more than one eligible payee

Cooperative cases – Cases carried jointly by the department and private agencies

Correctional institution – A prison or other institution for the legal confinement of persons who have violated penal law

Cost containment – Efforts on the part of administration to reduce the cost of services

Cross-reference case and number – The name and case number of a basic case whose record contains pertinent information and documentation concerning individuals included in another basic case.

Delinquent child – A child over 7 and under 16 years of age who violates any law or municipal ordinance or commits any act which, if committed by an adult, would be a crime.

Dependent child – A child who is in the custody of, or wholly or partly maintained by, an authorized agency, institution, or other organization of charitable, correctional, or reformatory character.

Destitute child – A child under the age of 6 who, through no neglect on the part of his/her parent, guardian or custodian, is needy, homeless, or in state of want or suffering due to lack of sufficient food, clothing, shelter, or medical or surgical care.

Direct grant – An allowance given directly to a client by either cash or check

EBT – Electronic Benefit Transfer (EBT) is an electronic system that enables a government agency to transfer benefits, such as food stamps, or unemployment payments, to recipients through a debit card. All states in the U.S. use an EBT system.

Fair hearing – An opportunity to show that a decision made by a government agency is wrong. A fair hearing may be conducted if one is requested by the applicant or client and deemed necessary by a government agency or department. The commissioner of social welfare appoints a referee to conduct the hearing. The referee is empowered to subpoena witnesses, administer oaths, take testimony, and compel the production of all records relevant to the hearing. Hearings are private and open only to interested parties, witnesses, counsel, and representatives of the state department of social welfare and the department of welfare. The proceedings and testimony are recorded. The referee submits his or her findings to the commissioner of social welfare who renders the decision on the case. Decisions are binding, and public welfare officials must comply.

Family home (for adults) – Home of a relative or close friend in which a client resides and where the arrangement for board and care is not a commercial one. Ordinarily, payment would not exceed cost of food and shelter. There would be no charge for service and no element of profit.

Federal participation – The part of the total grant that the federal government reimburses the state

Forms of charge – LC- Local Charge; PSC- Presumptive State Charge

Foster care – Care of a destitute, neglected, or delinquent child in an institution or a home other than that of the child's parents designated by an agency.

Foundling – A deserted infant whose parents are unknown

GED – The General Educational Development (GED) testing program enables adults who are at least 16 years old to earn a high school equivalency diploma. Individuals must pass an array of tests in writing, social studies, science, math, and reading.

Geographic caseload – A caseload with fixed territorial boundaries

Guardian – One who legally has the care and management of the person, the estate, or both, of a child while he or she is a minor

Head Start Program – A national program for promoting school readiness operated by the United States Department of Health and Human Services. Head Start provides educational, nutritional, health, and social services to low-income children and their families. One of the primary focuses of Head Start is helping preschoolers develop early reading and math skills.

Indirect grant – An allowance made payable to a third party for goods or services given to a client

Intake worker – A worker who usually has the first contact with a client and conducts some form of assessment of suitability for services.

Job Corps – A free education and vocational training program offered by the U.S. Department of Labor

LEP – Limited English Proficiency (LEP) refers to individuals who are unable to communicate effectively in English because it is not their primary language.

LIAB – The Life Insurance Adjustment Bureau (LIAB) is a service organized by the Metropolitan, Prudential, and John Hancock life insurance companies. The LIAB advises all public and private social agencies in the U.S. in adjusting, serving, liquidating insurance policies and assisting in securing benefits from policies carried by clients.

Lien – A legal claim on property as security for a debt or charge

Lodger - A person who occupies a room in a client's home and pays rent but prepares meals or eats elsewhere

Mandatory clients – Involuntary clients who are required to engage in services, usually by an agency policy, a court, an employer, or a family member

Master file – The system maintained in welfare centers and other public assistance granting divisions where the names of applicants and clients with whom the particular welfare center or division has had any contact are recorded. Its purpose is to properly identify applicants and clients and prevent of duplication of public assistance.

Medicaid – A federal health program for individuals and families with limited resources of low incomes. State agencies manage Medicaid and state and federal governments fund it jointly.

Model – A representation of reality

Mortgage – A pledge or security of particular property for the payment of a debt or the performance of some other obligation

Neglected child – A child under the age of 16 who is without proper guardianship. A child whose parent, guardian, or person with whom the child lives, due to cruelty, mental incapacity, immorality, or depravity is unfit to care properly for such child. A child who is under unlawful or improper supervision, care, custody, or restraint by any person, corporation, agency, or other organization or who wanders about without lawful occupation or restraint. A child who is unlawfully kept out of school; or whose parent, guardian, or custodian neglects or refuses, when able to do so, to provide necessary medical, surgical, institutional, or hospital care for such child. A child found in any place that is in violation of the law; or who is in such condition of want or suffering, or is under such improper guardianship or control, as to injure or endanger the morals or health of the child or others.

Non-geographic caseload – A caseload without territorial boundaries within the territory covered by the case unit (partially non-geographic caseload); or within the territory covered by the welfare center (completely non-geographic caseload)

Nonrecurring expenditures or grant (special grant) – A special allowance granted, when necessary, to meet a specific need as it arises

Non-reimbursable – Used for any item for which the local government bears the total cost and does not receive reimbursement from the state department of social welfare

NORC – A Naturally Occurring Retirement Community (NORC) is any building or neighborhood in which many senior citizens live. In general, NORC's were not constructed as retirement or senior housing areas. Instead, they are areas where older adults have migrated or have lived for many years.

Norms – The rules of behavior that are generally accepted by the dominant group in society

Not accepted – A statistical definition denoting that, after a field investigation of an application for public assistance, the applicant is determined to be ineligible

Other eligible payee – (only in a composite case) Eligible payees other than the responsible head

Pending case – A statistical definition denoting that an application for public assistance is under field investigation but no decision to accept or reject has yet been reached

Petitioner – A complainant in a legal action

Physical handicapped child – A person under the age of 21, who by reason of physical defect or infirmity, whether congenital or acquired by accident, injury, or disease, is or may be expected to be totally to partially incapacitated for education or for remunerative occupation. Physically handicapped children do not include the blind and the deaf.

Poverty guidelines – Issued by the U.S. Department of Health and Human Services, and used for administrative purposes, such as determining financial eligibility for federal assistance programs

Poverty threshold – Based on statistical information provided by the United States Census Bureau and used to calculate the number of people in poverty

Private home for the aged – A not-for-profit institution caring for the aged that is incorporated. The state department of social value inspects and approves it.

Private nursing home – A home privately owned and operated for profit and offers room, board, and bedside care for compensation to persons 16 years of age and older. All private nursing homes are inspected and licensed. A certificate valid for one year, stating the maximum bed capacity is issued to the facility if it is approved.

Proration – The method used to calculate the amount of the recurring grant if it is to be issued for a period other than the regular payment period

Public assistance roll – Used by the disbursing section of the division of accounting to record the public assistance checks prepared in accordance with the authorization of the welfare center or division

Rapport – A sense of good harmony between the client and the caseworker

Readjustment (of cases) – The reallocation of individual caseloads within a case unit, where caseloads are maintained on a non-geographic basis, with no resultant change in the total number of caseloads in the unit

Realignment – A general reallocation of the cases of an office resulting in an increase or decrease of the total number of caseloads or case units. All of the territory administered or just a portion of thereof may be involved.

Re-applicant – An applicant who has previously applied to the department for public assistance

Reassignment (of cases) – The temporary allocation of cases of an uncovered caseload, without statistical transfer, to other caseloads in the same unit in order to provide coverage for all cases administered. When no investigator is assigned or when the investigator formerly assigned has been absent from the assignment for any reason in excess of thirty days the caseload is considered uncovered.

Re-budgeting – Re-computation of each item of the budget as required when there is a change in the family situation involving needs or income or whenever the budget schedules of the department are revised

Reclassification – The action taken when an active case receiving one type of assistance is found eligible for another type of public assistance, when it is necessary to change the form of charge, or a combination of the two. Portions of one case may be reclassified from one type of assistance to one or more types of public assistance. Pending cases may be reclassified, when necessary, at the point of acceptance.

Redelivery – The action taken when a public assistance check returned undelivered by U.S. Postal Service is delivered to the client personally either in the welfare center or in his/her home

Redistribution - The reallocation of cases of individual caseloads within a case unit, where the caseloads and case unit are maintained on a geographic basis, resulting in changes in the caseload boundaries but with no change in the total number of caseloads in the unit

Reimbursable – Any expenditure for which part or the entire amount is repaid to the local government by the state, by the federal government through the state, or both

Residence club and residence center – Congregate living arrangements providing private rooms and common dining room facilities for persons needing protective care and desiring social contacts

Resistance – Behavior on the part of the client that appears to oppose the worker's efforts to deal with the client's problem. This is usually a sign of the client's pain associated with the work.

Respondent – A person in a legal proceeding who occupies the position of a defendant

Responsible head – In a single case this refers to the eligible payee. When both the husband and wife are appointed as eligible payees, the husband is the responsible head. In a composite case, the responsible head is the eligible payee who takes primary responsibility for the family group.

Restricted payment – A payment made to a third party for goods or service provided to a client or a grant or allowance given to a client with instructions that it be used for a specific purpose

Schizophrenia – A serious mental illness whose contributory factors include environment, genetics, and psychological and social processes. Symptoms appear as auditory hallucinations, bizarre delusions, paranoia, and disorganized speech. This disorder mainly affects cognition, but also contributes to emotional and behavioral problems.

Self-determination – The inherent right and need of every client to make their own decisions

Service interview – Any interview with a client that involves requests for public assistance/services, questions, concerns, or information submitted to a caseworker

Single case – A case with either a family or individual where there only exists one payee

Skill – A specific technique or behavior used by a caseworker performed while working a case

SNAP – Supplemental Nutrition Assistance Program (SNAP); official designation for the governmental Food Stamp Program

Source – The Source Credibility theory states that people more likely to be persuaded when a source presents itself as credible, for example Bochner and Insko found that people were more likely to trust a sleep expert than a non-sleep expert, on matters surrounding sleep.

SSI – Supplemental Security Income (SSI) is a monthly arrangement provided by the Social Security Administration for the benefit of low-income and disadvantaged individual

Status – Classification of a given case

Stop authorization form – Form that is used when public assistance has been discontinued

Sources

American Psychiatric Association. (2000). Diagnostic and statistical manual of mental disorders (4th ed., text rev.). Washington, DC: Author.

Azrin, N. H., Donohue, B., Besalel, V. A., Kogan, E. S., & Acierno, R. (1994). Youth drug abuse treatment: A controlled outcome study. Journal of Child & Adolescent Substance Abuse, 3, 1–16.

Center for Substance Abuse Treatment. Enhancing Motivation for Change in Substance Abuse Treatment. Rockville (MD): Substance Abuse and Mental Health Services Administration (US); 1999. (Treatment Improvement Protocol (TIP) Series, No. 35.) Chapter 4—From Precontemplation to Contemplation: Building Readiness. Available from:
http://www.ncbi.nlm.nih.gov/books/NBK64968/

Gambrill, Eileen. 2006. Social work practice: A critical thinker's guide. 2d ed. New York: Oxford Univ. Press.

Hepworth, Dean H., Ronald H. Rooney, Glenda Dewberry Rooney, Kim Strom-Gottfried, and Jo Ann Larsen. 2006. Direct social work practice: Theory and skills.7th ed. Belmont, CA: Brooks Cole.

Huff, D. (2005). The social work history station. Retrieved August 4, 2010, from http://www.boisestate.edu/socwork/dhuff/xx.htm

National Institute of Mental Health of the U.S. Department of Health and Human Services Anxiety Disroders

Shulman, Lawrence. 2009. The skills of helping individuals, families, groups, and communities. 6th ed. Pacific Grove, CA: Brooks Cole Cengage Learning.

http://www.socialworktoday.com/archive/mayjun2008p16.shtml

http://psychcentral.com/disorders/sx13t.htm

http://www.arhp.org/publications-and-resources/clinical-fact-sheets/sexuality-
and-sexual-health

http://www.naswdc.org/practice/standards/sw_adolescents.asp#9

http://www.naswdc.org/practice/standards/NASWculturalstandards.pdf

http://psychcentral.com/lib/what-are-impulse-control-disorders/0001161

http://www.ninds.nih.gov/disorders/autism/detail_autism.htm

http://www.socialworkers.org/pubs/code/default.asp